CW01335404

BATTLESHIPS
of the Grand Fleet

Below: *Indomitable* on her first trial runs shortly after leaving Fairfield Shipyard on completion in 1908. The three even-height funnels and long forecastle gave *Indomitable* and her two sisters *Invincible* and *Inflexible* a magnificent profile.

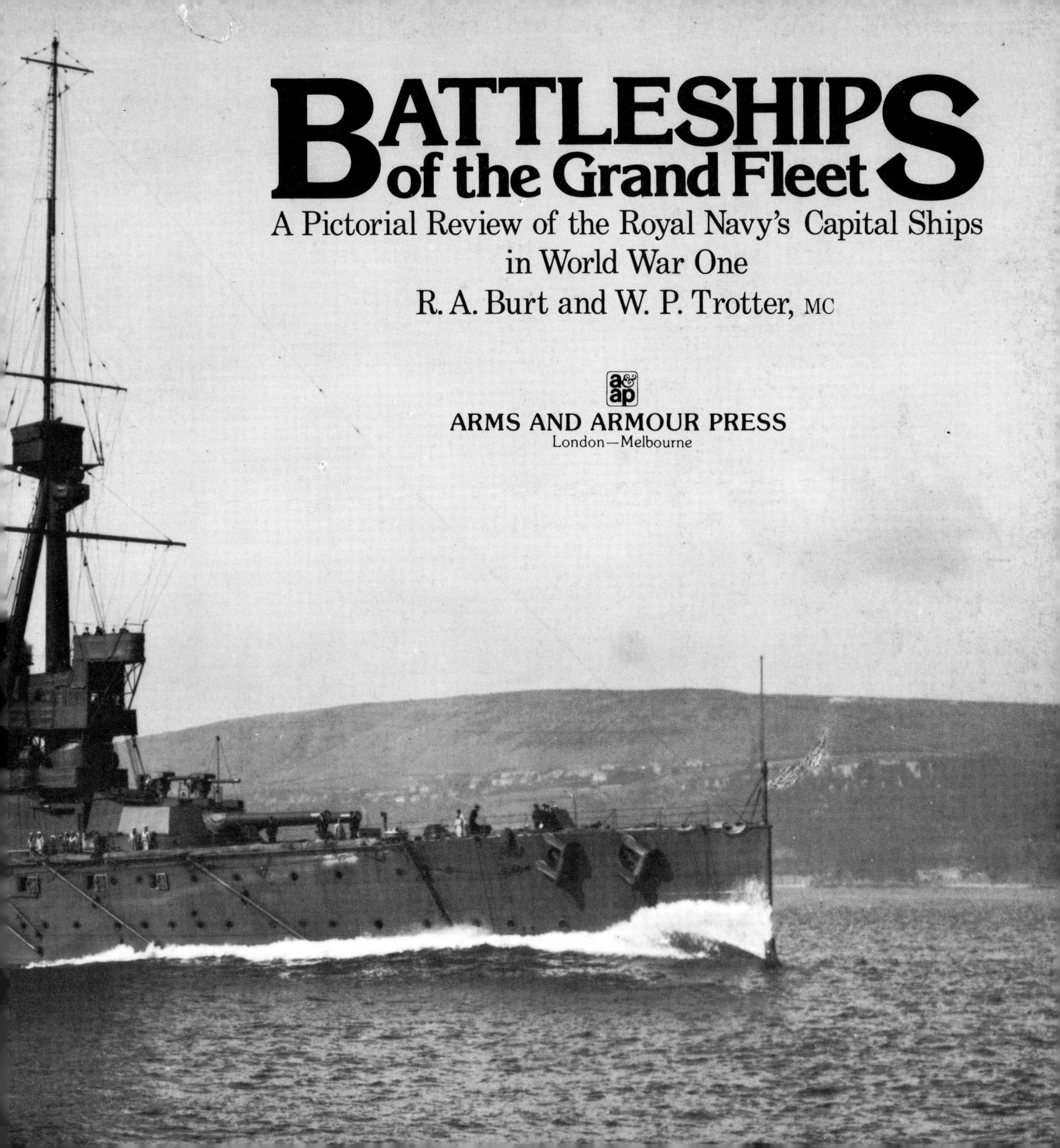

Battleships of the Grand Fleet

A Pictorial Review of the Royal Navy's Capital Ships in World War One

R. A. Burt and W. P. Trotter, MC

ARMS AND ARMOUR PRESS
London—Melbourne

ental Limited.
Introduction

Published in 1982 by
Arms and Armour Press,
Lionel Leventhal Limited.
Great Britain:
2–6 Hampstead High Street,
London NW3 1QQ.
Australasia:
4–12 Tattersalls Lane,
Melbourne, Victoria 3000.

© R. A. Burt and W. P. Trotter, 1982
© Lionel Leventhal Limited, 1982
All rights reserved. No part of
this publication may be reproduced,
stored in a retrieval system, or
transmitted in any form by any means
electrical, mechanical or otherwise,
without first seeking the written
permission of the copyright owner
and of the publisher.

British Library Cataloguing in Publication Data:
Burt, R. A.
Battleships of the Grand Fleet
1. Great Britain. *Royal Navy*
2. Battleships — History — Pictorial Works
I. Title   II. Trotter, W. P.
623.8′252′0941   VA454
ISBN 0-85368-550-9 (cased)
ISBN 0-85368-563-0 (paperback)

Layout by Anthony A. Evans.
Typeset by Typesetters (Birmingham) Limited.
Printed and bound in Great Britain by
William Clowes (Beccles) Limited.

The line drawing of HMS *Bellerophon* was made from plans held at the National Maritime Museum, London.

At the end of the nineteenth century, Great Britain possessed without doubt the largest and most powerful steel battlefleet the world had ever seen. Her navy had the capability to bring to action simultaneously the world's next two most powerful fleets with, theoretically, every chance of winning such a confrontation — such was the strength of the Royal Navy during this period. In the twenty years since 1880, basic British ship design changed from favouring a low freeboard ship, with large guns of different sizes mounted on unprotected barbettes (for example, the *Admiral* class vessels *Sans Pareil* and *Victoria*, 1882–1886), to a uniform design with high freeboard and guns that were protected by armoured hoods or turrets as they were later called (*King Edward VII* class, 1903 estimates).

Until 1892, the armour protection for vessels had consisted of compound iron plates which, in some cases, were to a maximum thickness of 20in. Their great weight confined the armour protection to the citadel of the ship. However, with the appearance of the new Krupp process,[1] by 1900 the British battleship was sporting a mere 9-inch thick armoured belt, which was more than equal to the 18 or 20 inches used previously. The great saving in weight that the Krupp process allowed, in most cases enabled the new ships to be fitted with wider belts. Thus the strake could now run past the citadel, if required, protecting the ends of the ship, which made for a better vessel, capable of withstanding punishment as well as delivering it. By 1903, 27 ships had been built with this protective plating. Usually, they were in classes of at least six vessels, forming homogeneous squadrons that could operate in any part of the globe.

The Royal Navy was content to rest with this situation, but in 1903 articles began to appear in several authoritative naval journals, concerning a type of ship that could carry an all big gun armament. There was a surge of interest in this concept, particularly after the 1903 edition of *Jane's Fighting Ships* published an article on the subject, written by Vittorio Cuniberti, a renowned Italian naval constructor. In his paper "An Ideal Battleship for the British Navy", he explained in great detail how such a vessel should be laid out and armed with the largest guns possible. The idea was not pure speculation on Cuniberti's part, for the figures he presented were feasible. He envisaged a vessel displaying some 17,000 tons, with a speed of 24 knots, and armament comprising twelve 12in guns. This theory was not new and had been propounded often by certain

---

[1] An all-steel plate was covered in animal charcoal to enhance its carbon content, and then passed through various heating and cooling processes. This technique hardened the face of the plate and considerably increased its resistance to shell impact.

staff members of the British Admiralty. Sketches and notes on the subject could be found stretching back as far as 1881, when Nathanial Barnaby (Chief of Naval Construction) had rejected such a novel design on the grounds that the increased size would make the project too costly. An additional obstacle lay in the established prejudices of the Board of Admiralty at that time, who were not prepared to change their notions of battleship design and make such a bold move.

The Admiralty viewed the resurgence of interest in the concept with a mixture of concern and discontentment because, with the public eye being drawn increasingly to the debate, questions that arose from articles such as Cuniberti's would eventually have to be answered. The Board of Construction knew only too well that such a vessel would make their existing fleet obsolete almost overnight. British battleships in service or still on the stocks were armed with a mixture of gun sizes, consisting of four 12in guns for main armament with an intermediate battery of ten 9.2in and a secondary backup of 6in pieces and would be hardly a match for a vessel with a proposed armament of up to twelve 10in or twelve 12in guns. It had been obvious for some years that a ship of this type would be built eventually. The rapid pace of technology together with a growing awareness that, in future, battles at sea would be fought at ever-increasing ranges — which was one of the lessons learnt from the recent confrontation between the Japanese and Russian fleets at Tshushima in May 1905 — conspired in favour of 'all big gun armed' ships. The arguments for and against the type would have to be discussed in great detail before building could commence. Apart from the cost of the project and the implications for the rest of the British fleet, the Admiralty had to consider the effect such a move might have on her position as the world's foremost sea power. This was one of the most compelling arguments against the type, for if Britain started to build and other navies followed suit — as they certainly would — and matched her rate of construction, the supremacy that the Royal Navy enjoyed would be lost. It might be possible for Britain to gain a clear lead over her rivals from the start, but it was uncertain whether it could be maintained. The United States had shown interest in the idea and had drawn up her own programme, resulting in the laying down of the *South Carolina* class early in 1905. She carried eight 12in guns on the centreline but retained the usual reciprocating engines.

It was extremely fortunate for the British Admiralty that one of their own staff was quick to seize the opportunity to voice his own enthusiasm for such a revolutionary ship. Some three years previous he had set up a small committee to draw up plans towards such a project. The man with this foresight was Admiral John Fisher, or 'Jackie Fisher' as he was affectionately known, who was Commander-in-Chief of the Mediterranean Fleet at the time, a position he held until 1904. Admiral Fisher was to use his considerable influence in favour of quickly building a big-gunned vessel and, supported by his staff, he made the Admiralty aware of their position as leaders in ship design and impressed upon them the need to forge ahead in the development of this new concept. Fisher was made First Sea Lord in 1904, which gave him a prime position from which to give the board the designs that his staff had been drawing up over the past few years. Each design was studied in great detail until eventually, after modifications, one was accepted.

Some twenty five to thirty designs had been submitted to the board during several committee meetings, with final agreement on a ship armed with 12in 45-calibre guns displacing 17,900 tons in the legend load condition, an increase of 2,900 tons over previous battleships which were usually 15,000 tons in the same condition. Another of the design's major innovations was the introduction of turbine machinery instead of the usual reciprocating plant, a feature that had been common practice for the past three decades. There had been encouraging experiments with turbine machinery fitted in smaller vessels, and it was felt that the advantages of the system would outweigh any possible drawbacks. The turbines gave less vibration and more reliability at high speeds, a feature that was lacking in the older plant. Further advantages with turbines included: a great saving in weight; fewer working parts; greater ease of maintenance, which necessitated fewer crew to staff the gear; a saving in coal consumption at high speeds; and increased protection for the machinery, as it was placed lower in the hull. The entire machinery plant of the new ship weighed 1,990 tons compared with 1,800 tons in the *King Edward VII* class (16,350 tons), but gave a nominal 5,000shp extra. The new turbine machinery was the first to be installed in a ship of such a size. It was regarded as 100 per cent more reliable than the older reciprocating plant, a claim that was proved later during trials.

It was decided to name the new ship *Dreadnought*. She was laid down in October 1905 and completed in October 1906, truly a magnificent achievement in shipbuilding ability. *Dreadnought* was built under a veil of secrecy, but there had been inevitable leakages of details and such was the interest shown even before her completion that it seemed the whole world was waiting for the vessel to make her appearance. After her commission she was put through a lengthy series of trials in which she fulfilled all expectations. The results of her trials confirmed for the Admiralty Board their predictions regarding the future of the rest of the British fleet, not a single unit of which could meet *Dreadnought* in action on equal terms. If other nations followed the example of the United States and proceeded to build all big-gunned ships, Great Britain would not be able to contain them with her existing fleet. In short, *Dreadnought* sparked off an international shipbuilding programme. Germany and Japan were extremely quick to act. Japan placed orders for all, big-gunned vessels with British shipyards, as she had neither the know-how nor the technology to produce them herself, although by 1914 she would have remedied this situation. Germany, of course, had many natural resources, but lacked the advanced technology to build a ship such as *Dreadnought*. Nevertheless she started her own programme, although procrastinating until 1907 when the results of the trials of *Dreadnought* became public knowledge.

This brings us to the ships featured in this book, the mighty dreadnoughts, a name given to all battleships and battlecruisers built after *Dreadnought* herself. The 'super dreadnought' (a term coined by the press to describe the *Orions* with their increased armament) arrived in 1912 with the completion of the *Orion* class, which were armed with 13.5in guns mounted in pairs along the centreline. This was a large increase from the 12in guns that had been fitted in the preceding sixteen ships (*Bellerophon* class, *St. Vincent* class, *HMS Neptune*, *Colossus* class, *Invincible* class and *Indefatigable* class). Admiral Fisher initiated the increase in armament, thus keeping the Royal Navy well ahead of any rivals and giving their ships a much greater weight of broadside. By the outbreak of war in August 1914, Great Britain had managed to maintain supremacy over her major rivals both numerically and technologically, with Germany as the number one contender.

The Royal Navy had twenty-two battleships completed and ready for action plus ten battlecruisers. The latter was a new breed of ship that sacrificed armoured protection to allow a greater proportion of displacement to be allocated for a more powerful propulsive machinery installation, thus enabling the vessel to reach speeds in excess of the conventional cruiser; the battlecruiser could exceed 25/26 knots, while a conventional cruiser's top speed was approximately 23 knots. This powerful fleet of capital ships could, if necessary, be backed up with over forty pre-dreadnoughts, which were very powerful ships in their own right. There were also three battleships under construction in British dockyards for foreign navies, all of which were taken over by the Royal Navy on the outbreak of war; much to the disgust of their rightful owners, although the Admiralty had regarded this step as a necessity, in case the ships should fall into enemy hands after delivery. Also under construction were vessels armed with gigantic 15in guns and innovatory all oil-burning boilers. Approval for these two novel ideas had been initiated by Admiral Fisher. Ten ships had been planned with these features, but the second batch of five reverted to coal-burning in the original design (*Royal Sovereign* class). All were in an advanced state of construction when war broke out, with the first, *Queen Elizabeth*, being completed in January 1915.

GRAND FLEET CAPITAL SHIP PROGRAMME

Battleships:

Dreadnought	1 ship	1905
Bellerophon Class	3 ships	1906
St. Vincent Class	3 ships	1907
Neptune	1 ship	1908
Colossus Class	2 ships	1908/9
Orion Class	4 ships	1909
King George V Class	4 ships	1910
Iron Duke Class	4 ships	1911
Queen Elizabeth Class	5 ships	1912/13
Royal Sovereign Class	5 ships	1913

Battlecruisers

Invincible Class	3 ships	1907
Indefatigable Class	3 ships	1908
Lion Class	3 ships	1909/10
Tiger	1 ship	1911
Renown Class	2 ships	1915
Courageous Class	2 ships	1916
Furious	1 ship	1916

Germany, in comparison, had her own very strong force, consisting of seventeen dreadnoughts, fifteen of which were ready for action with two fitting out, plus six battlecruisers, one of which was fitting out. These could be supported by 23 pre-dreadnoughts if need be, although they were not on the same scale as the Royal Navy's vessels and were regarded as being of inferior design and in some cases only fit for shore patrol. Germany, too, had four more capital ships under construction. Three of them, *Hindenburg*, *Baden* and *Bayern*, were not completed until late 1916 early 1917, too late to see action at Jutland due to their slow rate of construction. The fourth ship, *Mackensen*, was still under construction at the end of the war and was never completed. While not on equal terms with the Royal Navy numerically, the German ships were considered excellent vessels, possessing great fighting qualities, and they posed the greatest threat to Britain's naval supremacy. The indisputable answer to the question of which nation constructed the best ships would only be provided by a face-to-face confrontation. A decider was clearly needed and was eagerly sought by both sides.

This long-awaited spectacle partially came about at the end of May 1916 at the Battle of Jutland when both fleets met. The action was scattered and started too late in the day, resulting in a frustrating, indecisive battle with the German ships slipping away in the night back to their base. Both fleets were badly mauled: Britain losing three battlecruisers (*Queen Mary*,

Invincible and *Indefatigable*) to Germany's one (*Lutzow*), plus a pre-dreadnought (*Pommern*). The German Navy never again attempted to meet the British Grand Fleet head-on, but kept them busy by posing a constant threat as a fleet in being.

The First World War was a period in which battleships, regardless of nation, ruled supreme. The dreadnought type was the ultimate deterrent, and these leviathans had little to fear. They were to enjoy this primary position through to the dispersal of the Grand Fleet in April 1919.

After the cessation of hostilities, the majority of Germany's dreadnoughts were interned at Scapa Flow and left to rot. The British Government was not sure what to do with the vessels, and the problem was only solved when the German crews scuttled their own ships in 1919. Meanwhile, America and Japan were both planning further gigantic capital ship programmes for vessels of immense dimensions, forcing Great Britain to follow suit and draw up proposals for vessels equal to any possible threat.

The United States began this latest phase in the 'battleship race' by laying down six *Indiana* class battleships and six *Constellation* class battlecruisers, all of which were over 40,000 tons and confidently predicted to give the United States supremacy of the seas. Not to be outdone, Japan had laid down six powerful 43,000-ton vessels by the summer of 1921.

Further proposals were put forward by all three nations for vessels of up to 48,000 tons, armed with 16- and 18-inch guns. By July 1921 the United States realized that she could not hope to foot the colossal bill needed to maintain such a programme, and she invited the largest naval powers in the world to a conference to discuss the limitation of naval armaments. Delegations from Great Britain, Japan, France and Italy attended the conference in Washington, which was chaired by the United States and lasted from November 1921 until February 1922. The building programmes of France and Italy were modest in comparison with those of the other three nations, as neither could afford the mammoth expenditure required for such ambitious projects. Space does not permit a full discussion of the bitter arguments that took place at the Washington Conference but, in general, it was finally agreed in principle that, with a few exceptions, all new construction should cease and older dreadnoughts and pre-dreadnoughts should be scrapped, leaving Great Britain and the United States approximately equal in strength regarding their existing fleets, followed by Japan, with Italy and France on an equal footing in fourth place. The total battlefleet tonnage was as follows: Great Britain, 580,450 tons; United States, 500,650 tons; Japan, 301,320 tons; France, 221,170 tons; Italy, 182,800 tons. Great Britain faired worse, mainly because she had to scrap many more serviceable warships. In the event, however, she was content to do so owing to the enormous cost of maintaining such a large fleet in peacetime. Capital ships were limited, and in 1922 the fleets looked thus: Great Britain, 22; United States, 18; Japan, 10; France, 7; Italy, 4. One of the main agreements of the treaty was that there should be a ten-year period in which no capital ships would be constructed, and this seemed to conform to a mutual concession.

The start of the Second World War in 1939 heralded an end to the battleship as the capital ship, even though there had been further construction programmes by the leading naval powers from 1936 onwards. The end of the ten-year period found Germany gearing up to full strength once more. This produced even more powerful vessels than those that had served in the First World War although gun sizes did not increase dramatically, the ships being better built and more heavily protected than before. The progress of war and its events took the ultimate power away from the sea and placed it in the air. Aircraft with their bombs and deadly torpedoes could sink a mighty battleship if left unprotected without adequate aircover of its own. Thus it was envisaged that the new capital ship would become the carrier and the most important vessel in the fleets of tomorrow. The once proud battlefleet was used as backup and, sadly, relegated to menial tasks such as convoy protection and shore bombardment.

After the Second World War, most of the world's warships came under close scrutiny from their respective navies, resulting in all but a few battleships being scrapped or laid up in mothballs. The last British battleship, *Vanguard*, was actually completed after the war in 1946 and was finally scrapped from the summer of 1960.

After hundreds of years of battleship construction, no more would these floating giants be seen bristling with guns, sailing the seas: the age of the battleship had finally come to rest. Now that this era is long gone and there has not been a British dreadnought-type battleship preserved for future generations to see, all one can do is look at photographs and wonder what it was like to watch row after row of these magnificent creations steaming in line. Towards that end this book contains many photographs from the time when the battleship was truly at its peak, namely from *Dreadnought* onwards. The photographs have been culled from the unique and complete collection of W. P. Trotter, M.C., who for over 70 years has collected warship photographs. It is fortunate that Mr. Trotter has had the foresight to preserve such an important archive, especially as the original glass negatives for many of the photographs no longer exist. I am sure that any person browsing through the pages of this book, either as a student of naval affairs or just an ordinary ship-lover, will discover many views he has not seen before and thoroughly enjoy these superlative photographs.

Mr. Trotter and I have been very selective in choosing the photographs. Our prime aim is to show the splendour of the vessels to the full, in the hope that even the layman might be impressed. A set of reference tables has been included to enhance the book and, hopefully, be of some assistance to the novice. If you enjoy this book as much as we have enjoyed compiling it, then it will have fulfilled our aims and served a purpose in keeping alive the memory of the once mighty dreadnought.

R. A. Burt, 1982

Forecastle deck

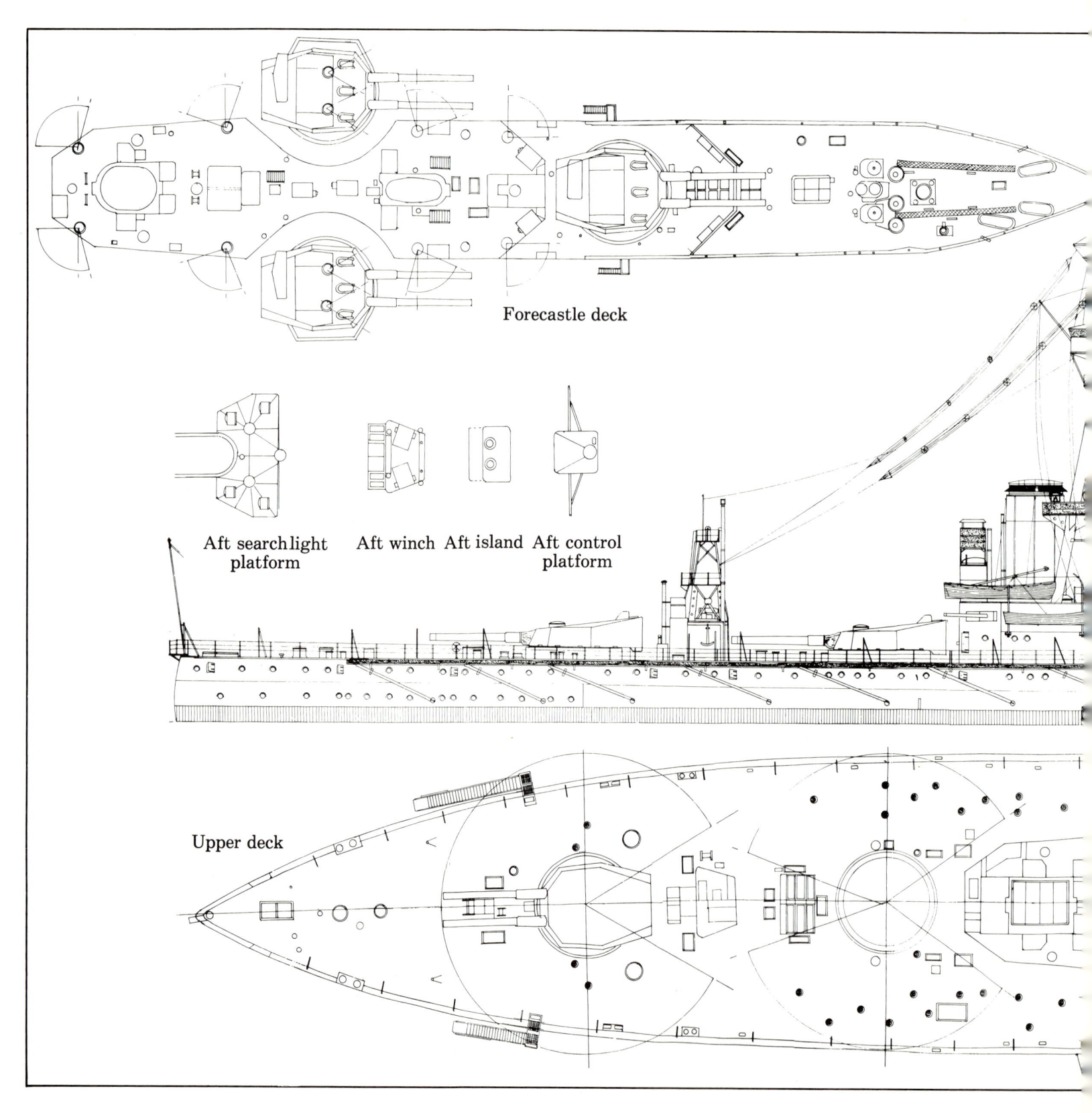

Aft searchlight platform   Aft winch   Aft island   Aft control platform

Upper deck

Boat stowage

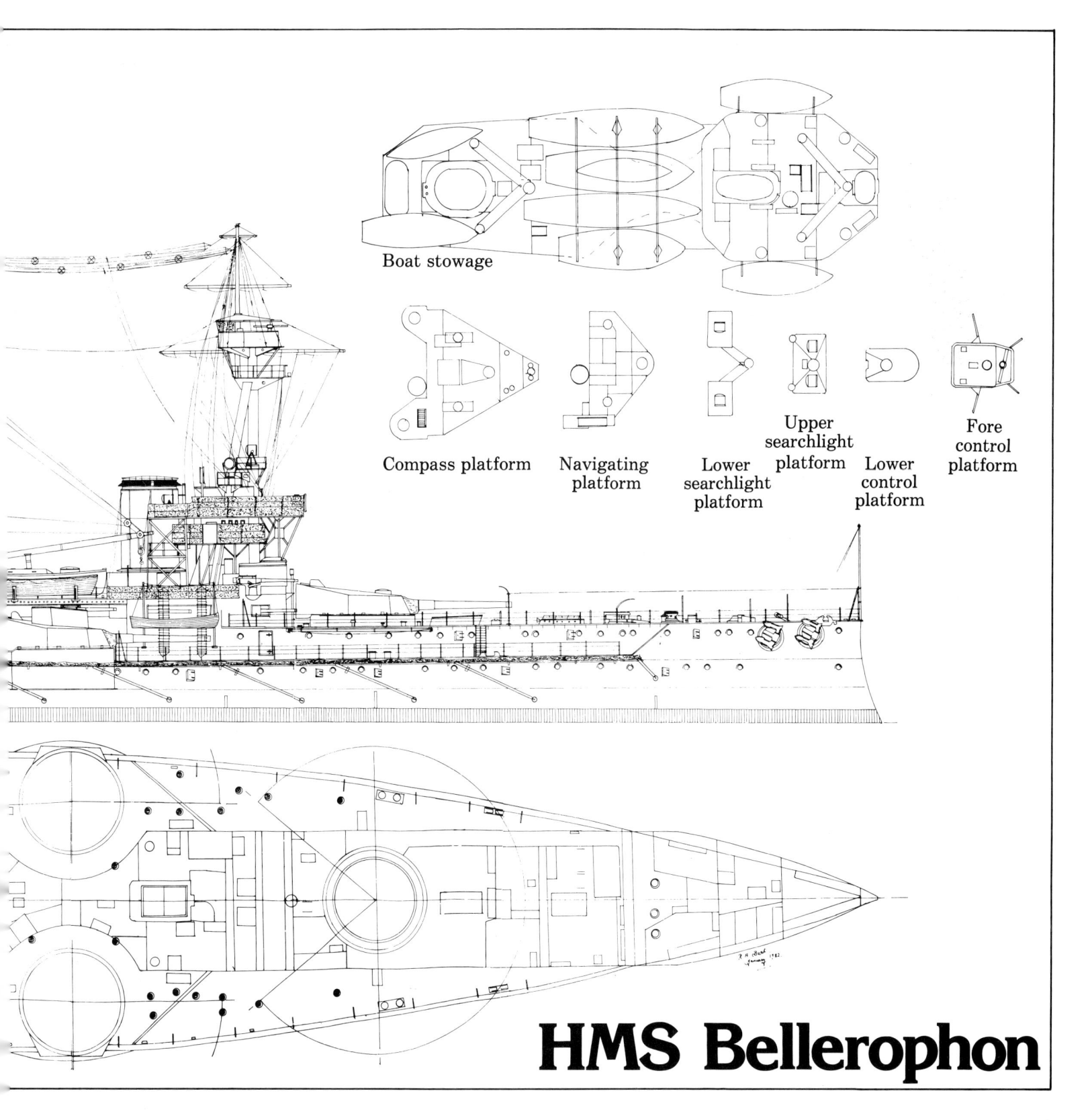

Compass platform   Navigating platform   Lower searchlight platform   Upper searchlight platform   Lower control platform   Fore control platform

HMS Bellerophon

DREADNOUGHT

Builder(s): Portsmouth Royal Dockyard
Laid down: 2 October 1905
Launched: 10 February 1906
Completed: October 1906

Displacement
Normal condition: 18,120 tons
Deep load: 20,730 tons

Dimensions
Length: 520ft (waterline); 527ft (overall)
Beam: 82ft 1in
Draught: 26ft 6in (normal); 20ft 7½in (deep load)

Armament (as completed)
10-12in 45-calibre
28-12pdr (18cwt)
1-12pdr (8cwt) field-gun
5 machine-guns
5-18in torpedo tubes

Armour protection
Main belt: 11in-7in amidships
Upper belt: 8in
End belts: 4in-6in
Bulkheads: 8in
Barbettes: 11in-8in-4in
Turrets: 11in-12in-3in
Conning tower: 11in
Main deck: 1¾in
Middle deck: ¾in
Lower deck: 1½in-2in-3in
Inclines: 2¾in
Anti-torpedo protection: 2in-4in screens

Machinery
Parsons direct-drive turbines with four screws
18 Babcock and Wilcox boilers
Engined by Vickers Shipbuilders
23,000shp for speed of 21 knots

Fuel and endurance
900 tons of coal (normal); 2,900 tons (maximum)
Endurance: 6,620 miles at 10 knots

Complement
700 (1907)

Fate(s)
The world's first 'all big gun' battleship, *Dreadnought* was sold for scrap in 1921.

Note: All endurance figures were achieved with oil fuel supplement.

Left: The stern of *Dreadnought*, taken after her trials in 1906. Note the small main tripod. The anti-torpedo nets have not yet been completely positioned on ship.

Top right: A port view of *Dreadnought* in the Spithead Roads, fully dressed for review by King Edward VII, 1907. To the left of the ship's bows is the wash from a submarine, whose commander was probably having a good look at the giant vessel. The Royal Yacht *Alexandra* can be seen on the right.

Below: *Dreadnought* at the Fleet Review in July 1914. This photograph shows her appearance shortly before the outbreak of war. She carries no mast on the main tripod aft, and shields are fitted around the 12-pounder guns in 'A' turret. *Dreadnought*'s basic appearance remained unchanged throughout her entire service, unlike many of her predecessors, which were fitted with extra bridge levels and searchlight towers, for example, as will be seen in the following pages.

INVINCIBLE CLASS

Name of ship:	*Invincible*	*Inflexible*	*Indomitable*
Builder(s):	Armstrongs, Elswick	John Brown Shipyard	Fairfield Shipyard
Laid down:	2 April 1906	5 February 1906	1 March 1906
Launched:	13 April 1907	26 June 1907	16 March 1907
Completed:	March 1908	October 1908	June 1908

Displacement
Normal condition: 17,420 tons
Deep load: 20,135 tons

Dimensions
Length: 560ft (waterline); 567ft (overall)
Beam: 78ft 8in
Draught: 25ft 5in (normal); 29ft 7in (deep)

Armament (as completed)
8-12in 45-calibre
16-4in 45-calibre
5-machine-guns
5-18in torpedo tubes

Armour protection
Main belt: 6in
Bulkheads: 7in-6in
Barbettes: 7in-2in
Turrets: 7in
Conning tower: 10in
Main deck: ¾in-1in
Lower deck: 1½in-2½in
Anti-torpedo protection: 2½in

Machinery
Parsons direct-drive turbines with four screws
31 Babcock and Wilcox boilers (*Indomitable*);
Yarrow boilers (*Invincible* and *Inflexible*)
41,000shp for 25 knots

Fuel and endurance
1,000 tons of coal (normal); 3,000 tons (maximum)
Endurance: 6,310 miles at 10 knots

Complement
784

Fate(s)
Invincible was sunk at the Battle of Jutland on 31 May 1916 when her magazines blew up as a result of heavy shell fire from *Lützow* and *Derfflinger*.
Inflexible, scrapped from April 1922.
Indomitable, scrapped from August 1922.

Above: *Invincible* with her funnel bands as painted up in 1909/10. This photograph was taken sometime between 1910 and 1912 and shows the rangefinder drums, which are visible on the faces of both fore and main tops. Her appearance has changed little since completion. *Invincible* was classed at first as an 'armoured cruiser' of exceptional quality, with the term 'battlecruiser' not coming into usage until 1912/13.
Top left: *Invincible* at Malta in 1913/14. As will be seen, the anti-torpedo nets have been removed and the wings of the forward bridge extended. These wings could be removed if necessary. The three sister-ships were quite easy to tell apart during this period, with *Invincible* the only unit not to have her forward funnel raised. There were also mast differences.
Top right: A superb shot of *Inflexible* entering Valetta Harbour in 1914. She was second flagship of the Battlecruiser Squadron, which was serving with the Mediterranean Fleet at the time. Her fore funnel has been raised and she is still carrying four yards on her forward mast. Note the tall topgallants fitted to both fore and aft masts. The blast screens fitted to 'A' 12in gun turret are clearly visible; they were also placed on 'X' turret. These were meant to protect the gun crew from the blast of the 4in armament located in the bridges.
Right: *Indomitable* in 1913, allowing a clear view of the extension fitted to the compass platform and its supporting struts below. Her 4in blast screens were removed sometime late in 1913 or early 1914, shortly after this photograph was taken.

13

Top left: *Indomitable* visiting Malta in 1913/14. The fore funnel has been raised 15ft above the other two in an attempt to keep the bridge free from smoke and excessive heat while steaming at sea. The problems caused by smoke can be seen clearly in the earlier photograph of the vessel.
Centre left: A unique view of *Inflexible* (left) and *Indomitable* on North Sea patrols, c.1915. Note that *Inflexible* still has her anti-torpedo nets.
Below: A rare shot of *Superb* during manoeuvres, 1916. Note her bridge-work, which has been greatly increased, and the searchlight arrangement around the top part of the foremast. The 4in secondary guns forward have had their ports plated over to afford some protection to the crews serving them. About half-way up the mainmast are 'anti-rangefinder baffles'. *Superb* is followed by *Temeraire*, to the right of the picture, with units of the *St. Vincent* class behind her.
Right: *Temeraire*, 1911. No changes have been made to her appearance since completion in 1909. This is a superb view and shows the gun layout very clearly. *Temeraire* has two bands on each funnel, *Bellerophon* had none and *Superb* carried two on the aft funnel.

BELLEROPHON CLASS

Name of ship:	*Bellerophon*	*Temeraire*	*Superb*
Builder(s):	Portsmouth Royal Dockyard	Devonport Royal Dockyard	Vickers Shipbuilders
Laid down:	3 December 1906	1 January 1907	6 February 1907
Launched:	27 July 1907	24 August 1907	7 November 1907
Completed:	20 February 1909	15 May 1909	9 June 1909

Displacement
Normal condition: 18,596 tons
Deep load: 22,540 tons

Dimensions
Length: 522ft (waterline); 526ft (overall)
Beam: 82ft 6in
Draught: 27ft 6in (normal); 31ft 4in (deep load)

Armament (as completed)
10-12in 45-calibre
16-4in 45-calibre
4-3pdr
2 machine-guns
3-18in torpedo tubes

Armour protection
Main belt: 10in-9in-8in-7in-5in
Bulkheads: 8in-4in
Barbettes: 10in-9in-5in
Turrets: 11in-12in-4in-3in
Conning tower: 11in
Main deck: ¾in-3in
Middle deck: 1¾in-3in
Lower deck: 1½in-4in
Anti-torpedo bulkheads: 1in-3in

Machinery
Parsons direct-drive turbines with four screws
23,000shp for speed of 20.75 knots
18 Babcock and Wilcox boilers (*Bellerophon* and *Superb*); Yarrow boilers in *Temeraire*

Fuel and endurance
900 tons of coal (normal); 2,648 tons (maximum)
Endurance: 5,720 miles at 10 knots

Complement
729-845

Fate(s)
Bellerophon, scrapped from 1922.
Temeraire, scrapped from 1922.
Superb, scrapped from 1923.

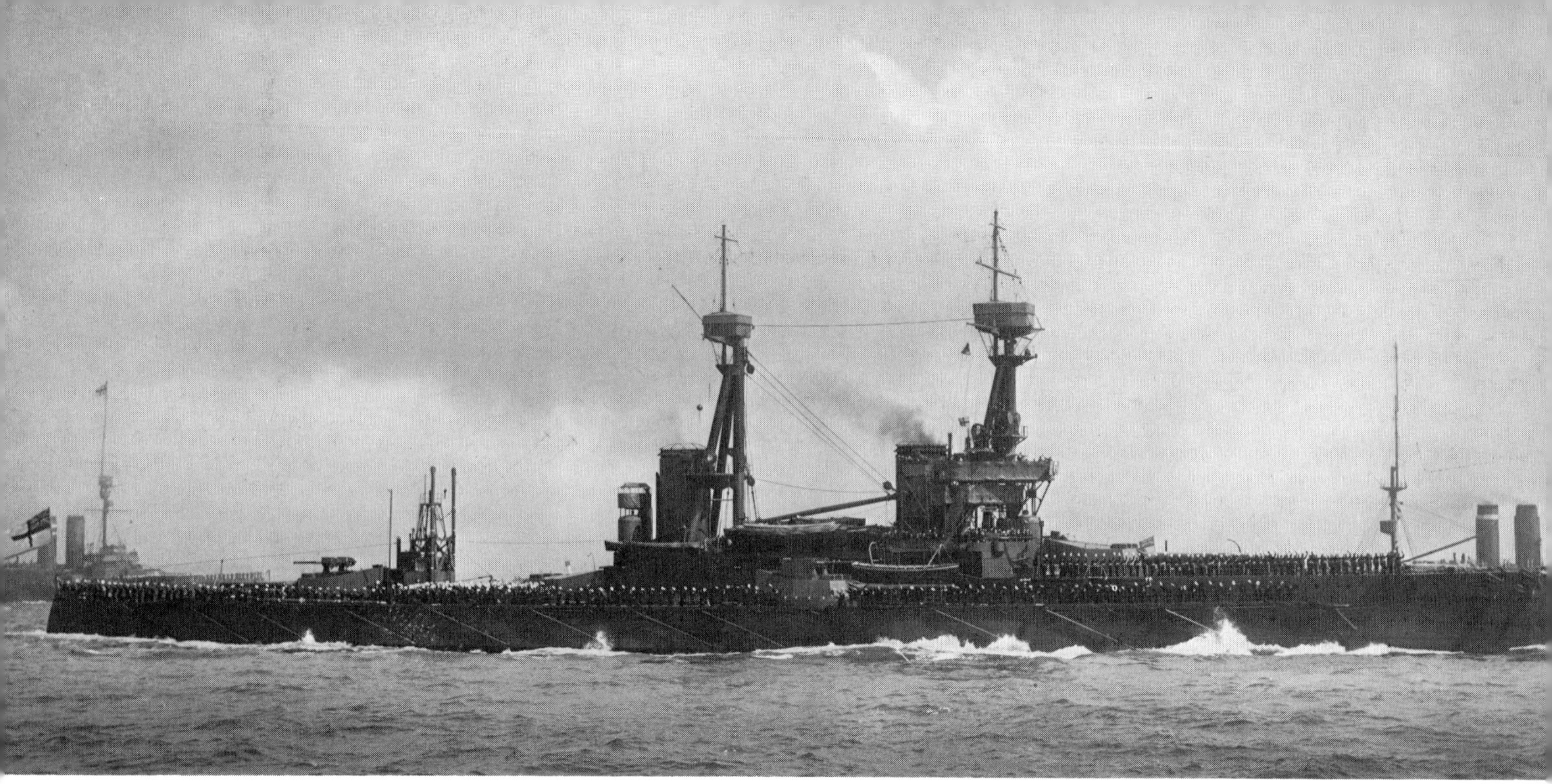

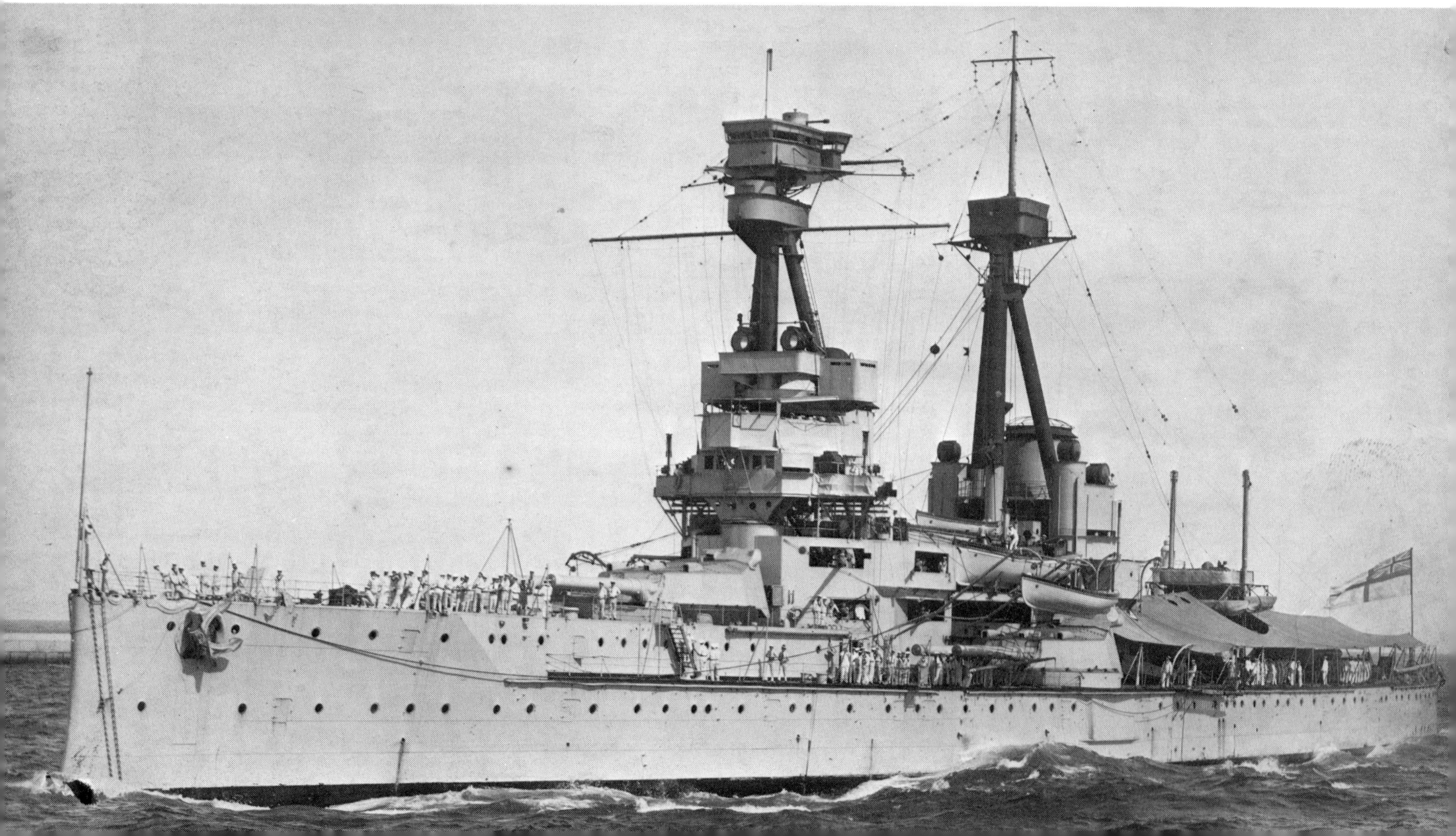

Top left: The name ship of her class, *Bellerophon* attending the Fleet Review at Spithead in July 1914. She is seen here passing the King (George V), with her complement raising their caps in salute. Note the bridge build-up, with the searchlight platforms placed around the mast.
Below: *Temeraire* serving in the Mediterranean as a training ship for cadets, 1920/21. It is worth comparing this view with that showing her as fitted in 1911 to see just how many changes and additions have been made. Compared with the earlier view, the ship now has a heavy appearance with the extra bridge levels and large tops. Note that the additions to the bridge have been constructed from sheet metal and not the usual canvas that was fitted throughout the war.
Top right: *Superb* entering Valetta Harbour, Malta in April 1919. She had been relieved as Fleet Flagship of the Mediterranean by *Iron Duke* in March of that year. The vessel is displaying all her wartime modifications: her rather heavy superstructure and large control tops, the prominent searchlight towers around the second funnel and her distinctive funnel cap which had a rather flatter top than those fittings in her sister-ships. The reduction in height of the aft island is easily viewed in this photograph.
Centre right: The launch of *St. Vincent*, 10 September 1908. Displacement figures at launch always varied among ships of the same class; for example, *St. Vincent* was 6,580 tons total, while her sister *Collingwood* was 7,930 tons. This variation was due to the different rates of construction between shipyards. Some shipbuilders were quicker than others at fitting equipment in the vessel before the launch date.
Below: *St. Vincent* as completed, looking very much like the previous class of *Bellerophons* except for the narrower fore funnel and distinctly larger second funnel. Another identification point between the two classes was that the *St. Vincents* had shorter topmasts and longer topgallants.

ST. VINCENT CLASS

Name of ship:	*St. Vincent*	*Vanguard*	*Collingwood*
Builder(s):	Portsmouth Royal Dockyard	Vickers Shipbuilders	Devonport Royal Dockyard
Laid down:	30 December 1907	2 April 1908	3 February 1908
Launched:	10 September 1908	22 April 1909	7 November 1908
Completed:	May 1909	1 March 1910	April 1910

Displacement
Normal condition: 19,400 tons
Deep load: 22,800 tons

Dimensions
Length: 500ft 3in (between perpendiculars); 536ft (overall)
Beam: 84ft 3in
Draught: 28ft 7in (normal); 30ft 6in (deep load)

Armament (as completed)
10-12in 50-calibre
18-4in
1-12pdr (8cwt) field-gun
5 machine-guns
3-18in torpedo tubes

Armour protection
Main belt: 10in-8in
End belts: 7in-2in
Bulkheads: 8in-5in
Barbettes: 10in-9in-5in
Turrets: 11in-8in-3in
Conning tower: 11in
Main deck: ¾in-1½in
Middle deck: 1¾in
Lower deck: 1½in-3in
Anti-torpedo bulkheads: 1½in-3in

Machinery
Parsons direct-drive turbines with four screws
18 Babcock and Wilcox boilers in *St. Vincent* and *Vanguard*; Yarrow boilers in *Collingwood*
Cruising turbines were abandoned in this class after problems with *Dreadnought* and *Bellerophon*
24,500shp for speed of 21 knots

Fuel and endurance
900 tons of coal (normal); 2,800 tons (maximum)
Endurance: 6,900 miles at 10 knots

Complement
756

Fate(s)
St. Vincent, scrapped from March 1922.
Collingwood, scrapped from March 1923.
Vanguard was a complete loss after an external magazine exploded — caused by a shell or a charge igniting — while she was anchored at Scapa Flow on 9 July 1917. There were only two survivors. The wreck was raised and scrapped in 1926.

Top left: *Vanguard* fitting-out at Vickers Shipyard, October 1909. Originally, she was to have been named *Rodney*, as the existing ship of that name (pre-dreadnought) had been earmarked for disposal in 1908. However, she was renamed *Vanguard* during March 1908 after the decision was made to retain *Rodney* for subsidiary service as a Submarine Depot.
Below left: *Collingwood* at the outbreak of war, with small additions to the bridgework and extra searchlights.
Top right: *St. Vincent* leaving for her first sea trials after completion, December 1909. All sisters of the class were practically identical except for small features, such as the slightly more prominent caging on the funnels of *Vanguard*. Funnel bands as painted up in 1909/10 were: *Collingwood*, one white band on second funnel; *St. Vincent*, two white bands on second funnel; and *Vanguard*, one red band on each funnel.
Below right: *St. Vincent* having her hull and propellers checked in dry dock, c.1912. Her plough-type bow is shown to advantage in this view.

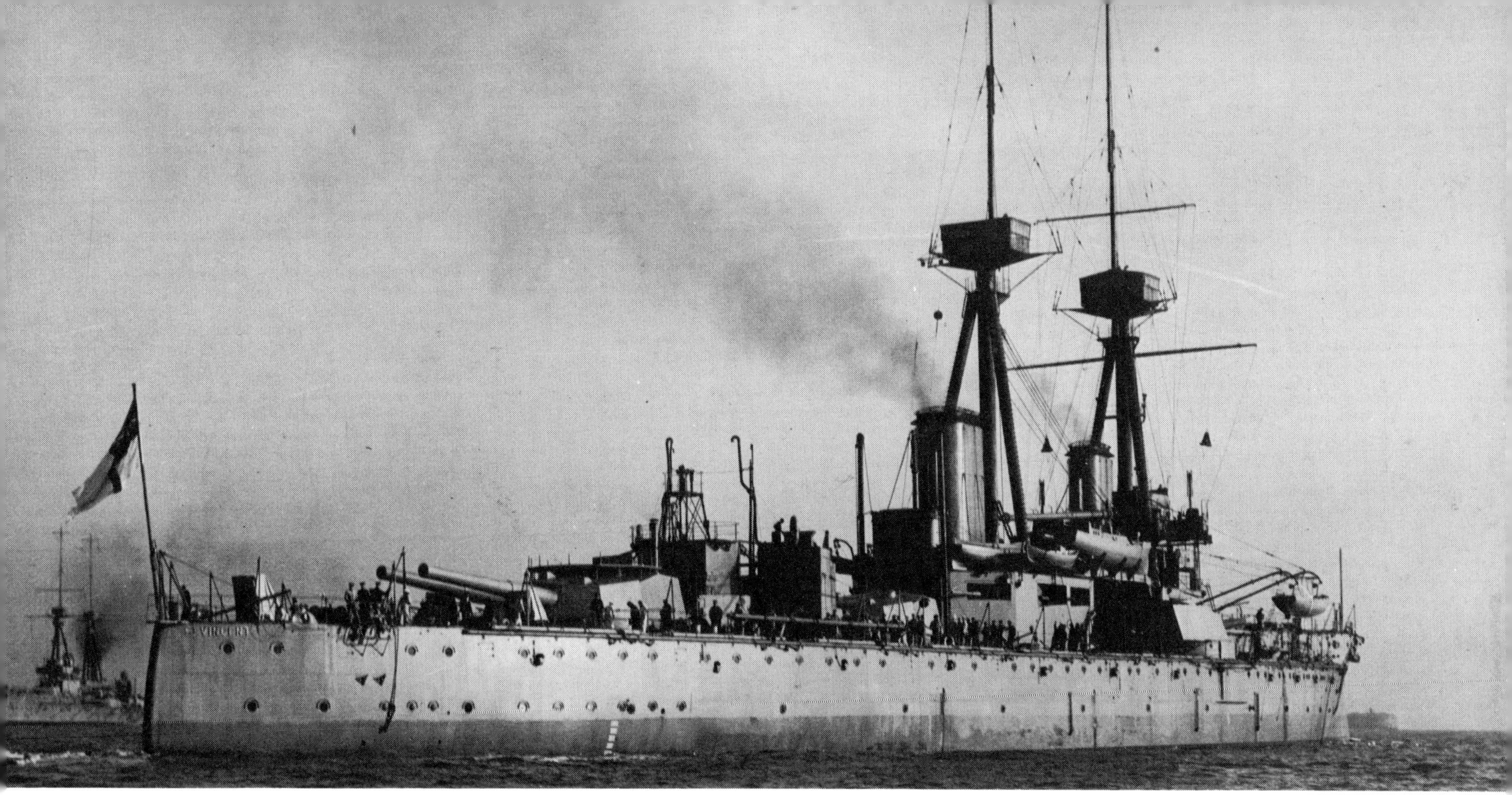

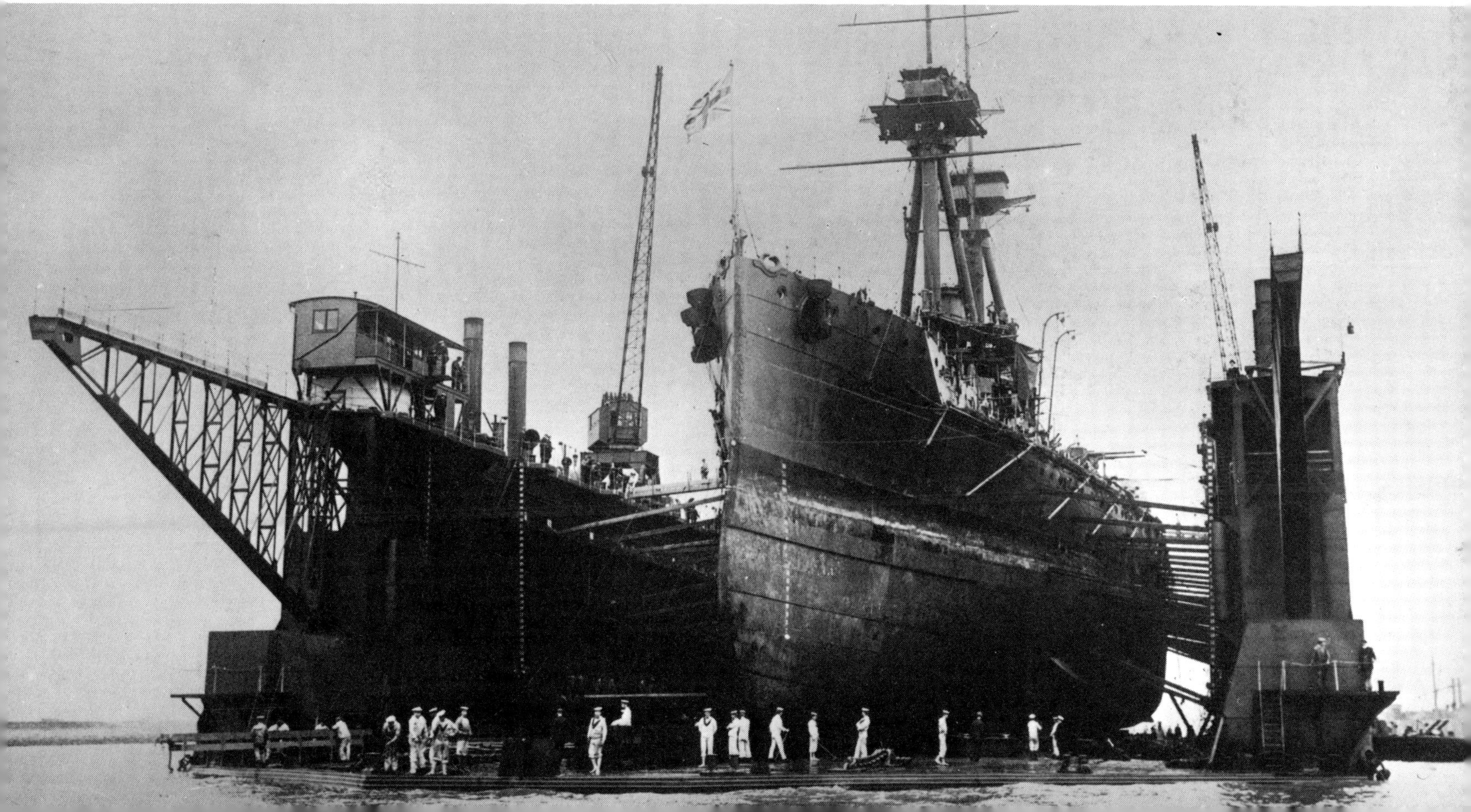

Left: *Vanguard* showing her stern in 1913. The photograph affords a good view of the after superstructure with the searchlight in the high position.
Top right: *Collingwood* at sea with *St. Vincent* ahead, c.1911/12. The 4in secondary gun arrangement is clearly visible in this shot, which was taken while *Collingwood* was serving with the Home Fleet.
Below right: *Vanguard*. Another of the splendid views in the series of pass-by shots taken at the Fleet Review, July 1914. Comparisons can be made with other battleships of the Grand Fleet attending this review. All have a steady build-up of bridgework forward, and all are painted in a very dark, Home Fleet grey.
Below: *Collingwood* at the Fleet Review, July 1914. *Collingwood* was a unit of the 1st Battle Squadron from August 1914 until June 1916 and then relegated to the 4th B.S. until the dispersal of the Grand Fleet in April 1919.

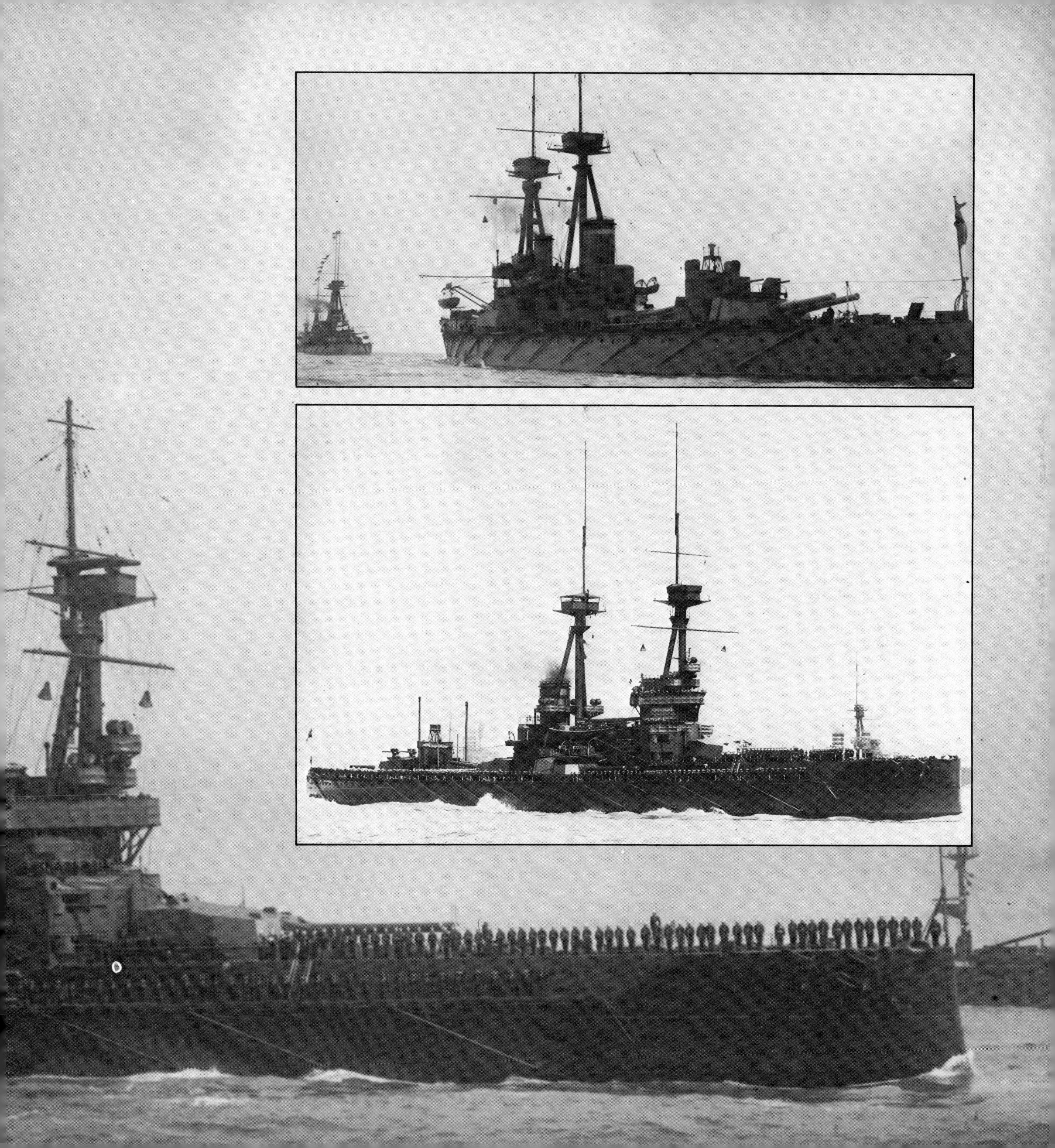

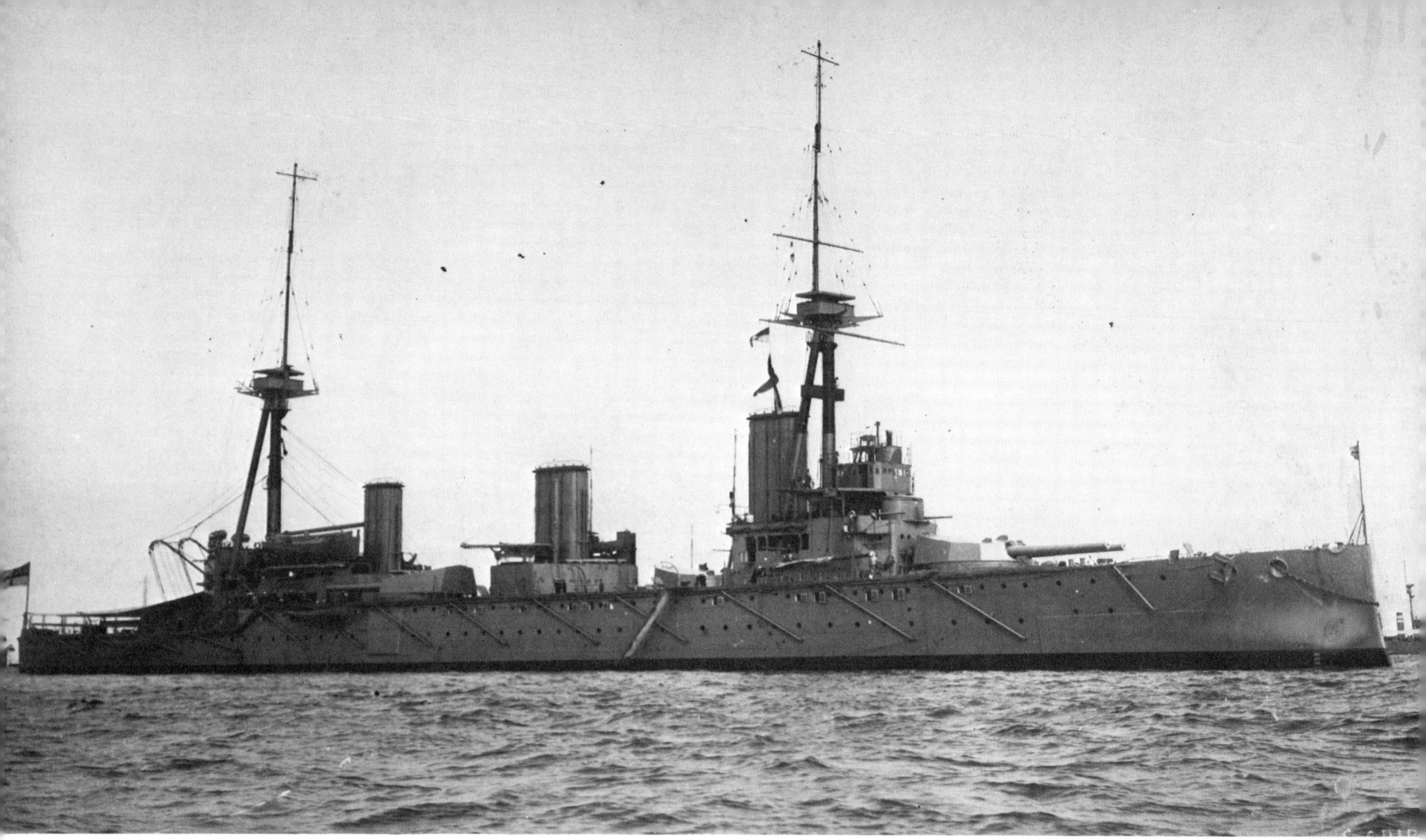

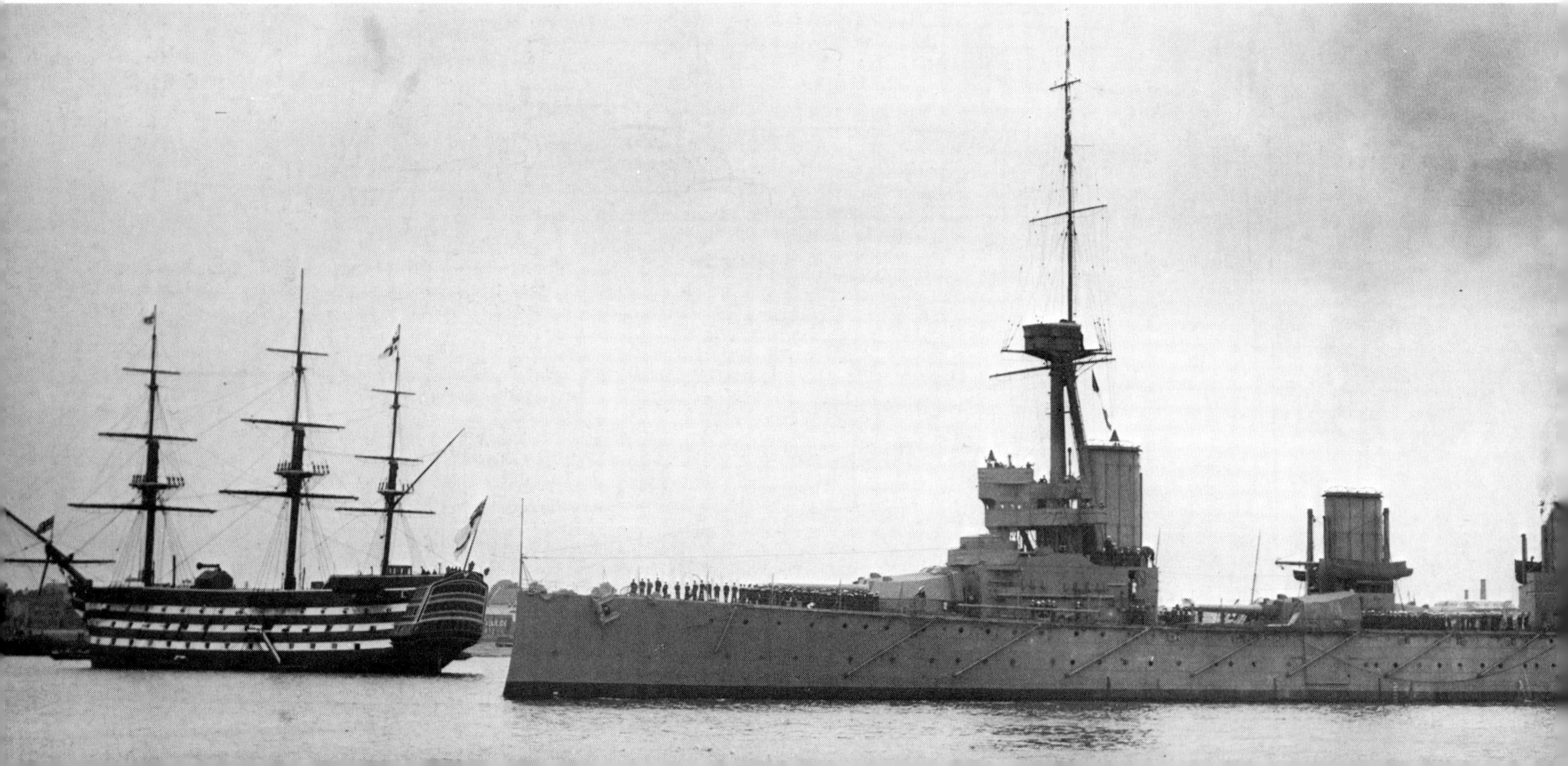

Left: The first of the 'Super Battle-cruisers', so called because it was thought that they greatly exceeded the *Invincible* class in all aspects. On completion they were soundly criticized when it was learnt that their protection was still totally inadequate. Apart from the funnel bands, of which *Indefatigable* (seen here) had none, the ships of the class could be identified by the low yard on the foremast, which was higher in *Australia* and *New Zealand*. The bridges in *Australia* and *New Zealand* were also different from that of *Indefatigable*, the former two being almost identical on completion.
Below left: *Australia* leaving Portsmouth Harbour in 1913. While based at Portsmouth, she was visited by HM King George V, who knighted Admiral Patey, the Australian Squadron commander, on the ship's quarterdeck.
Right: *New Zealand*, late 1917/early 1918, showing wartime modifications. The vessel now sports a heavy, enclosed bridge and unique searchlight arrangement around the centre funnel. Note the large control top forward with range and control tops below; the mainmast has no top.
Below right: *Indefatigable*, leaving Malta in the summer of 1914 when she was serving with the 2nd Battle-cruiser Squadron. Her anti-torpedo nets have been removed and extra searchlights fitted. The height of the after superstructure is well marked.

INDEFATIGABLE CLASS

Name of ship:	*Indefatigable*	*Australia*	*New Zealand*
Builder(s):	Devonport Royal Docks	John Brown Shipyard	Fairfield Shipyard
Laid down:	23 February 1909	23 March 1910	20 June 1910
Launched:	28 October 1909	25 October 1911	1 July 1911
Completed:	February 1911	June 1913	November 1912

Displacement
Normal condition: 18,750 tons
Deep load: 21,540 tons

Dimensions
Length: 555ft (waterline); 590ft (overall)
Beam: 80ft
Draught: 26ft 4in (normal); 29ft 4in (deep load)

Armament (as completed)
8-12in 45-calibre
16-4in 45-calibre
4-3pdr
1-12pdr
5 machine-guns
2-18in torpedo tubes

Armour protection
Main belt: 6in amidships
End belts: 4in-2½in
Bulkheads: 4in-3in
Barbettes: 7in-4in-3in
Turrets: 7in
Conning tower: 10in
Main deck: 1in
Lower deck: 1½in-2½in
Magazine screens: 2½in

Machinery
Parsons direct-drive turbines with 4 screws
31 Babcock and Wilcox boilers
43,000shp for speed of 25 knots

Fuel and endurance
1,000 tons of coal (normal); 3,170 tons (maximum)
Endurance: 6,690 miles at 10 knots; 3,500 miles at 18 knots

Complement
790-806

Fate(s)
Indefatigable was sunk at the Battle of Jutland on 31 May 1916. Heavy shells from the German battlecruiser *Von der Tann* struck her upper deck near 'Y' turret and her magazines exploded. There were two survivors.
Australia was scuttled under the Washington Treaty's Age Clause, off Melbourne, 23 April 1924.
New Zealand, scrapped from August 1923.

Below: *Australia* in July 1913. She was built for the Australian Navy by John Brown Shipbuilders in Scotland. Although *Australia* served with the Grand Fleet in the war, she was never made a gift to the Royal Navy like her sister *New Zealand*. Note the long extensions to the bridge forward.

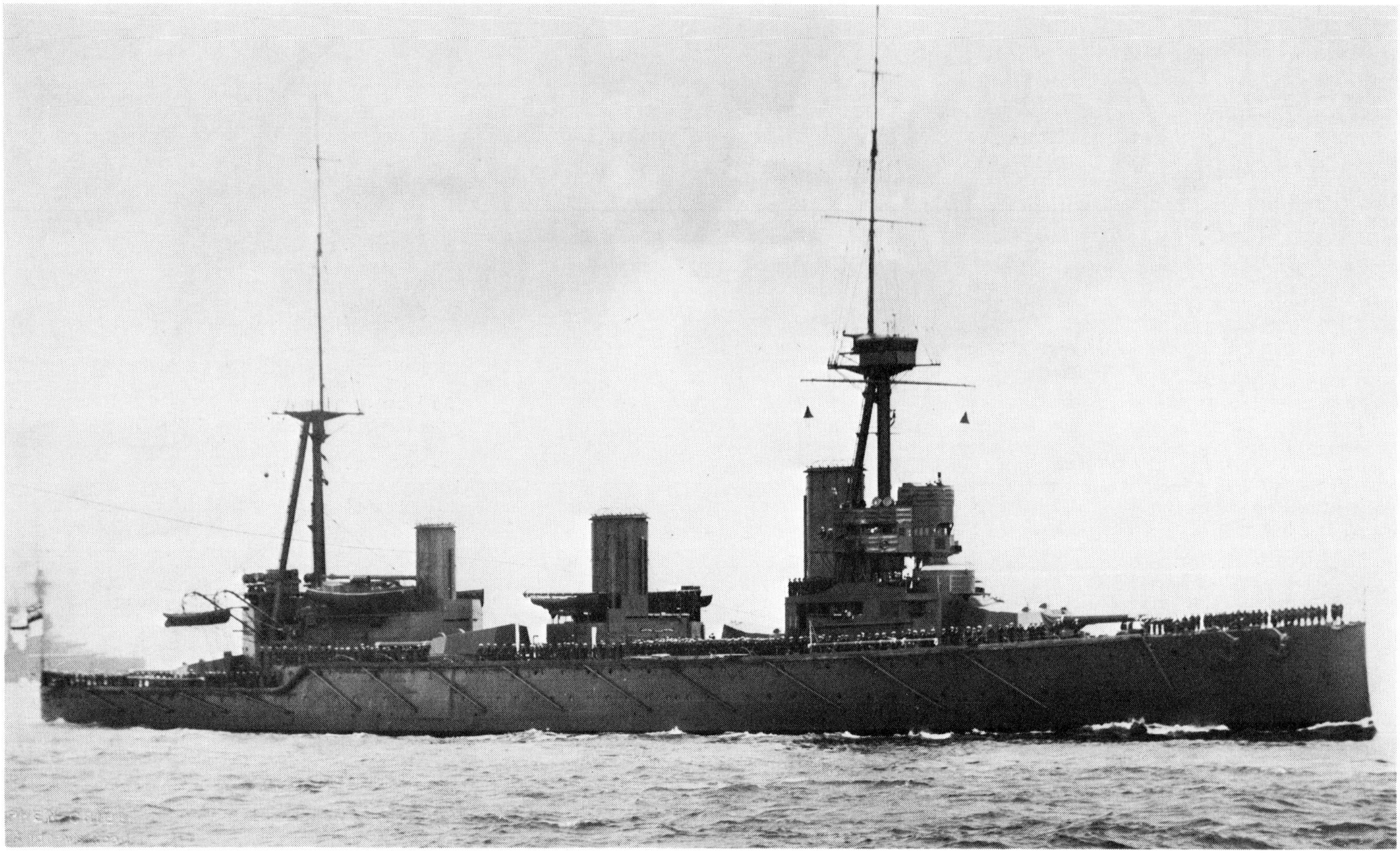

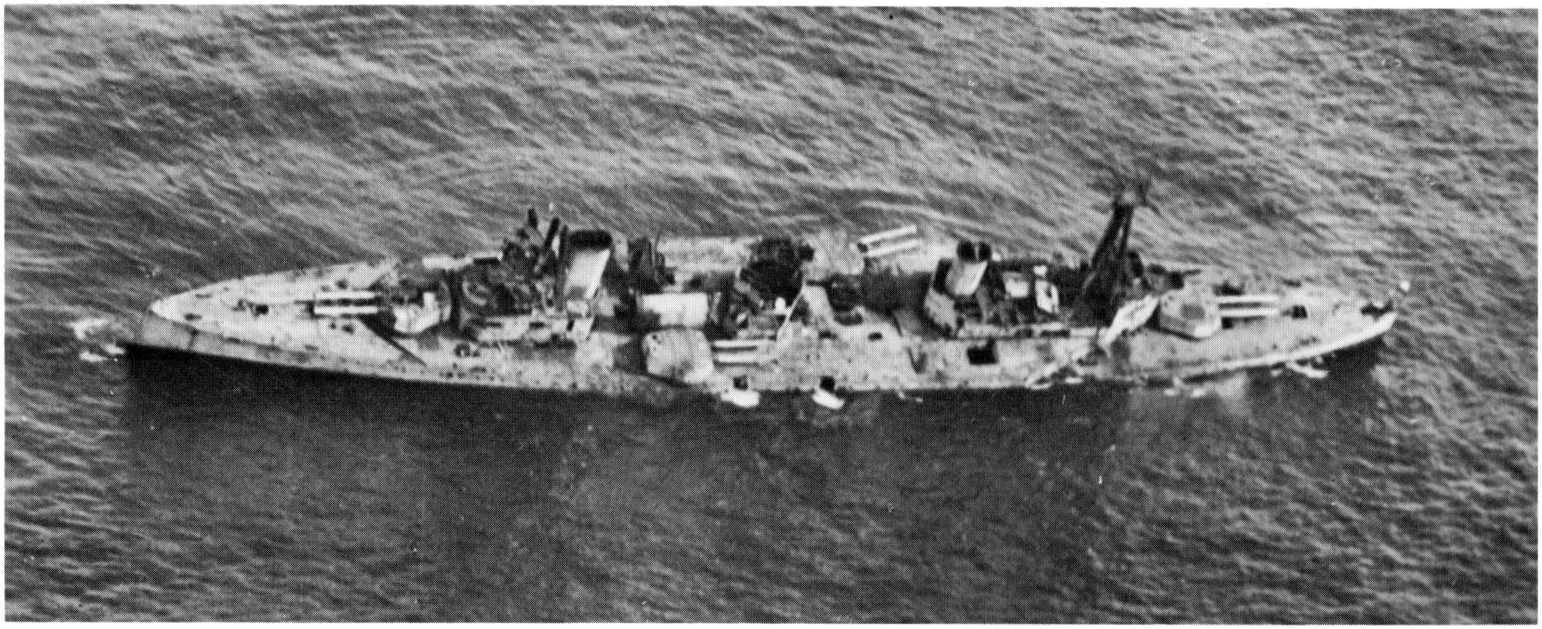

Top left: *New Zealand* passing the King at the Fleet Review on 20 July 1914, which was possibly the largest gathering of dreadnoughts ever seen.
Below left: On 12 December 1921 *Australia* was paid off into reserve at Sydney and remained there until being designated a victim of the Washington Treaty's Age Clause. From October 1923 she was in Sydney dockyard being prepared for disposal. The vessel was towed out through the Heads at Port Jackson, escorted by the Australian Squadron on the 12 March 1924. She was scuttled with honours 24 miles to the east of the port in 150 fathoms of water. The photograph shows *Australia* listing to port with her deck amidships awash. The tops of the masts have been cut down and all small fittings removed.
Below: *Hercules*, as completed, 1911. Although the funnels are of equal height, both *Hercules* and her sister *Colossus* had an unbalanced appearance due to the single, heavy tripod and rather large funnel forward. Like *Dreadnought*, this class had the reversed tripod, which was known to be a failure but nevertheless was fitted in both ships. Twin tripods were abandoned once more and, apart from *Neptune*, were never again fitted to a British dreadnought.

COLOSSUS CLASS

Name of ship:	*Colossus*	*Hercules*
Builder(s):	Scotts Shipbuilding	Palmers Shipbuilding
Laid down:	8 July 1909	30 July 1909
Launched:	9 April 1910	10 May 1910
Completed:	July 1911	August 1911

Displacement
Normal condition: 20,030 tons
Deep load: 23,266 tons

Dimensions
Length: 541ft 6in (waterline); 545ft 9in (overall)
Beam: 85ft 2in
Draught: 27ft (normal); 29ft 5in (deep load)

Armament (as completed)
10-12in 50-calibre
16-4in
4-3pdr (saluting)
3-21in torpedo tubes

Armour protection
Main belt: 11in-8in
End belts: 7in-2½in
Bulkheads: 8in-5in-4in
Barbettes: 10in-9in-7in-5in
Conning tower: 11in
Main deck: 1½in
Middle deck: 1¾in
Lower deck: 1¼in-4in
Anti-torpedo bulkheads: 1in-3in

Machinery
Parsons direct-drive turbines with 4 screws
18 Babcock and Wilcox boilers in *Colossus*;
18 Yarrow boilers in *Hercules*
25,000shp for a speed of 21 knots

Fuel and endurance
900 tons of coal (normal); 2,900 tons (maximum)
Endurance: 6,680 miles at 10 knots

Complement
778

Fate(s)
Colossus, scrapped from September 1928.
Hercules, scrapped from October 1922.

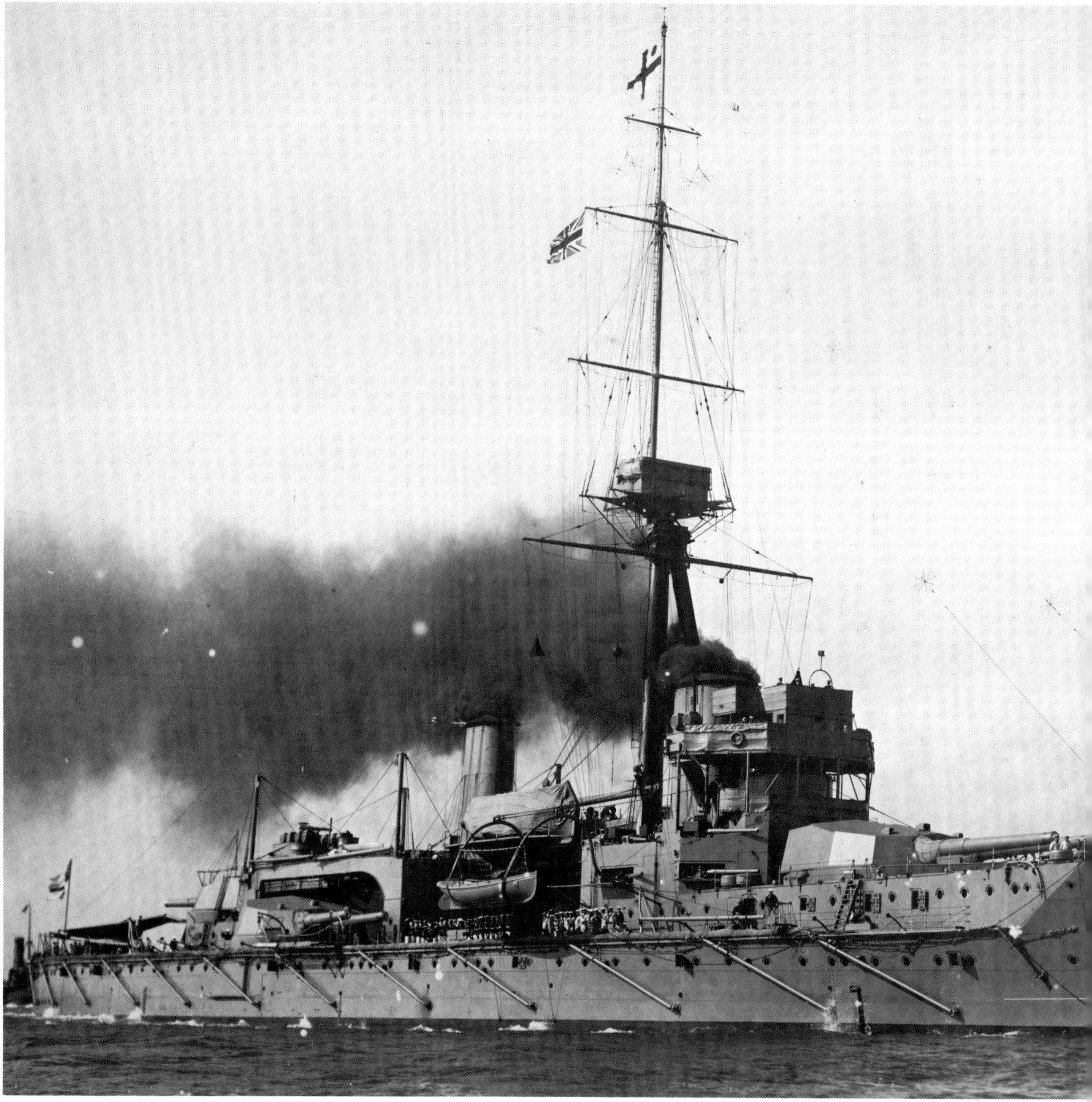

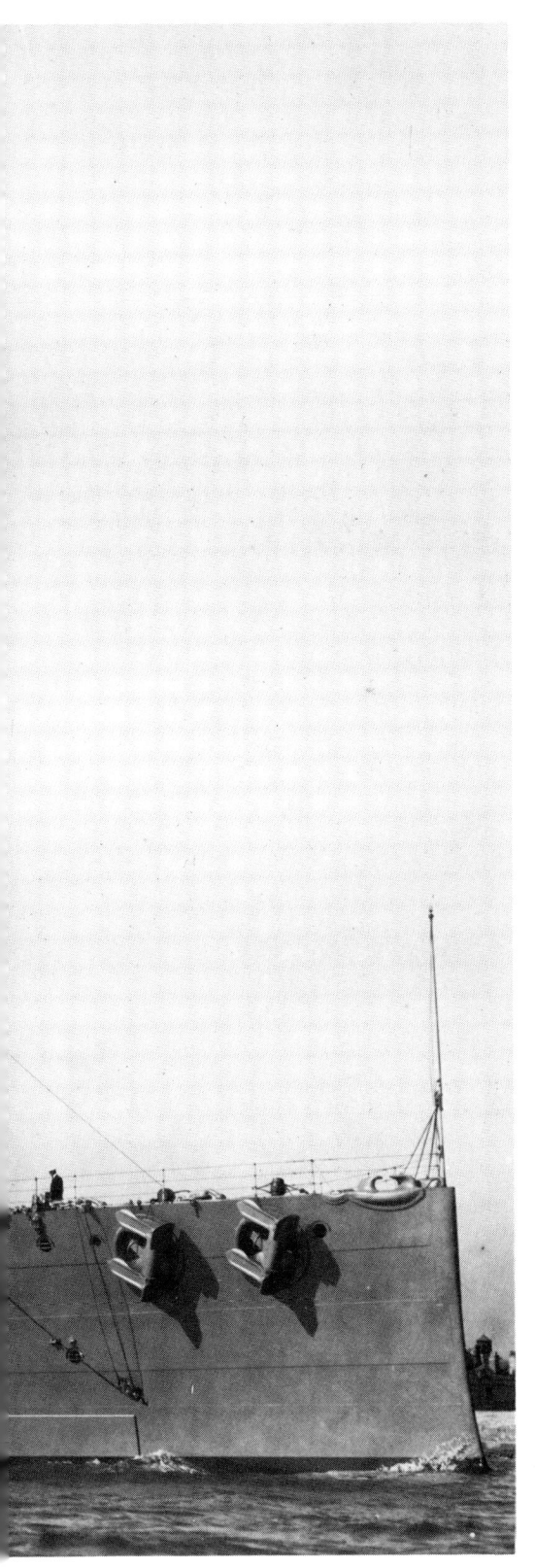

Left: A superb shot of *Hercules* as commissioned in August 1911. Note that the upper level of 4in secondary guns are uncovered. The searchlight layout is clearly visible, with twin fittings in the forward bridge and two pairs each port and starboard in the aft structure. Both *Hercules* and *Colossus* were completed with four yards on the topmast.

Top right: A port quarter view of *Colossus*, taken in 1912 shortly after completion. The after turrets are superimposed, a feature that *Colossus* was one of the first to enjoy. The searchlight layout on the after superstructure can be seen clearly.

Below right: *Hercules* opens fire with her 12in armament during battle practice. Unlike previous British dreadnoughts to date, no provision had been made for the wing 12in guns to fire on either beam. In the *Colossus* class the forward and aft superstructure was cut away to allow both beam turrets greater arcs of fire. This worked well in theory, but, in practice, when the guns fired across the decks, the position was placed under considerable strain. To alleviate the problem, these arcs of fire were only used when engaging the enemy.

30

Left, top: *Hercules*, 1912. In both *Hercules* and *Colossus* the standard magnetic compass position had to be moved to the aft structure from its usual position mounted on the forebridge because of the effect on the ships' magnetism produced by the oblique layout of the two wing turrets.
Far left, below: *Hercules* as completed, showing her general layout. The shot was taken when *Hercules* was acting as flagship of the 2nd Division of the Home Fleet.
Left, below: *Colossus* at the Fleet Review, 20 July 1914. She was a unit of the 1st Battle Squadron from 1912 until the outbreak of war in August 1914 when she joined the newly-formed Grand Fleet; the Home Fleet was dispensed with for the period of hostilities.
Above: *Colossus* in 1913, after her forward funnel had been raised by approximately 10ft in an attempt to reduce the smoke problems endured by personnel on the top and bridges.
Right: Another general view of *Hercules*, 1913, showing her raised funnel and white funnel band.

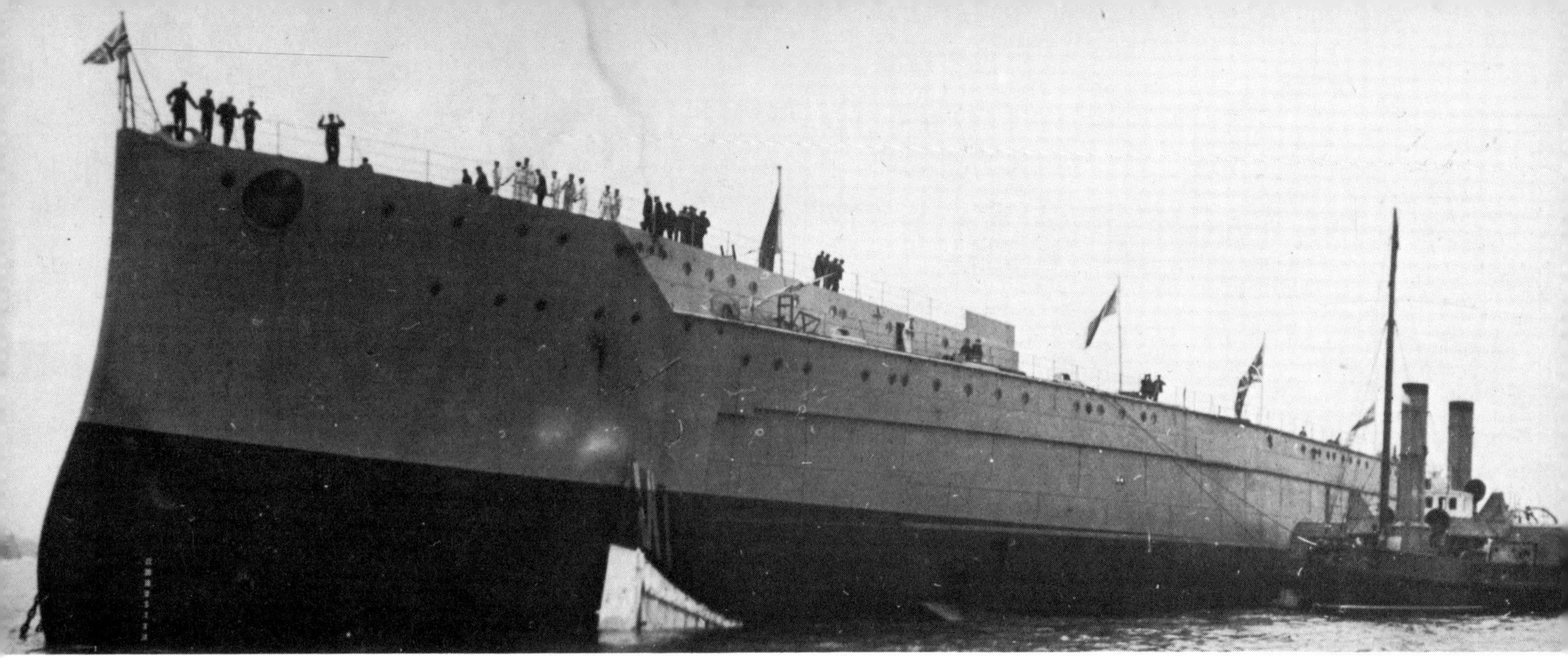

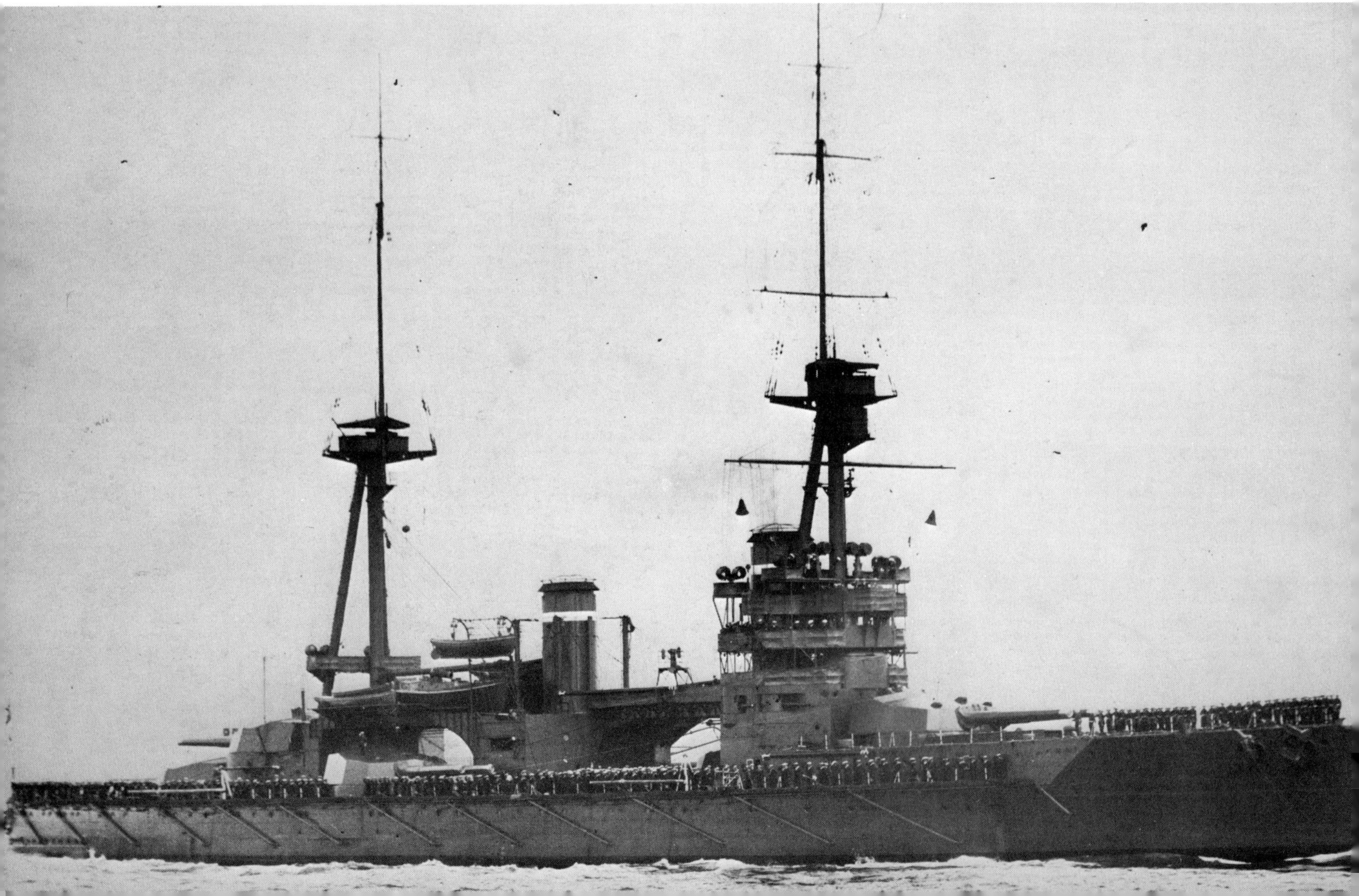

NEPTUNE

Builder(s): Portsmouth Royal Dockyard
Laid down: 19 January 1909
Launched: 30 September 1909
Completed: January 1911

Displacement
Normal condition: 19,680 tons
Deep load: 23,123 tons

Dimensions
Length: 510ft 1in (between perpendiculars); 546ft (overall)
Beam: 85ft
Draught: 28ft 6in (normal); 30ft 8in (deep load)

Armament (as completed)
10-12in 50-calibre
12-4in
1-12pdr (8cwt) field-gun
5 machine-guns
3-18in torpedo tubes

Armour protection
Main belt: 10in-8in
End belts: 7in-2½in
Bulkheads: 8in-5in-4in
Barbettes: 10in-9in-5in
Turrets: 11in-8in-3in
Conning tower: 11in-8in
Main deck: 1¼in
Middle deck: 1¾in
Lower deck: 1½in-3⅜in
Anti-torpedo bulkheads: 1¼in-3in

Machinery
Parsons direct-drive turbines with four screws
18 Yarrow boilers
25,000shp for speed of 21 knots

Fuel and endurance
900 tons of coal (normal); 2,710 tons (maximum)
Endurance: 6,330 miles at 10 knots

Complement
756, as commissioned

Fate(s)
Scrapped from September 1922.

Top left: *Neptune* being launched at Portsmouth on 30 September 1909. Her total displacement at launch was 7,139 tons, which compares favourably with her two half-sisters, *Hercules* and *Colossus* (7,325 tons for *Colossus*, 7,883 tons for *Hercules*).
Below left: *Neptune* taking her place in the line at the Fleet Review, July 1914. Her additions since completion are easily viewed here. Her new director control gear can be seen just below the foretop; she was the first British battleship to be fitted with this type of director, which was manufactured by Vickers. Notice the unique arrangement of searchlights around the bridge.
Top right: A starboard quarter view of *Neptune*, taken at Portsmouth Harbour shortly after her preliminary sea trials. Although a half-sister to the *Colossus* class, she was designed with better armour distribution and, in fact, sported a complete armoured strake from stem to stern. *Neptune* was the last British battleship to be fitted with twin tripods. A good-looking ship, she had equal-shaped funnels of the same height. Note the searchlight layout on the mainmast, and that all of the large boats, such as motor launches, are stowed after on the flying platform, while the smaller gigs and cutters are stowed forward. She carries three yards on the forward topmast, although an extra one was fitted later.
Below right: *Neptune* showing her funnel bands as painted up in 1911–12. Compare this view with the previous one and note how the forward top has been reduced in width. The four yards mentioned above can now be seen.

34

Far left: An excellent view of the twin superimposed 12in turrets aft in *Neptune*, 1911. This shot was taken during coaling operations and the gun muzzles have been covered to prevent dust from entering. The crew have obviously stopped work for a moment's breather and, no doubt, a well-earned cup of tea.

Left, top and centre: Two views of *Neptune* showing her increased funnel height, 1913. This alteration spoiled her classic appearance somewhat but was considered necessary to alleviate the smoke problems that occurred in so many of the early dreadnought designs.

Below: Battleships at war, c.1915. Various vessels of the Grand Fleet anchored at Scapa Flow ready for sea at a moment's notice. *Neptune* is in the foreground with *Colossus* behind. Units of the *Bellerophon* and *St. Vincent* classes are ahead of them.

Top right: *Neptune* at the outbreak of war in August 1914. Note the searchlight platforms fitted around the base of the mainmast.

Centre right: A rare view of *Neptune* taken late in 1918, showing wartime modifications. The forward flying deck has been removed and the searchlight arrangements greatly altered, with towers fitted around the second funnel. The new control top is very large, and the vessel now sports a funnel cap. Note that the ship has no topmasts except for a small fitting on the main tripod.

Below right: *Neptune* after the war, c.1919. Her funnel cap has been removed and extra searchlight towers fitted around the mainmast. In the background is either *Renown* or *Repulse*.

ORION CLASS

Name of ship:	*Orion*	*Conqueror*	*Monarch*	*Thunderer*
Builder(s):	Portsmouth Royal Dockyard	Beardmore Shipbuilders	Armstrong Shipbuilding	Thames Iron Works
Laid down:	29 November 1909	5 April 1910	1 April 1910	13 April 1910
Launched:	20 August 1910	1 May 1911	30 March 1911	1 February 1911
Completed:	January 1912	November 1912	February 1912	May 1912

Displacement
Normal condition: 21,900 tons
Deep load: 29,108 (1918)

Dimensions
Length: 576ft (waterline); 581ft (overall)
Beam: 88ft 6in
Draught: 27ft 6in (normal); 31ft 3in (deep)

Armament (as completed)
10-13.5in 45-calibre
16-4in 50-calibre
1-12pdr (8cwt)
4-3pdr (saluting)
5 machine-guns
3-21in torpedo tubes

Armour protection
Main belt: 12in
Upper belt: 8in
End belts: 6in-4in
Bulkheads: 10in-6in
Conning tower: 11in
Upper deck: 1½in
Main deck: 1½in
Middle deck: 1in
Lower deck: 1in-4in
Anti-torpedo protection: 1in-1¼in

Machinery
Parsons turbines driving four screws
18 Babcock and Wilcox boilers (*Orion*, *Conqueror* and *Thunderer*); Yarrow boilers in *Monarch*
27,000shp for speed of 21 knots

Fuel and endurance
900 tons of coal (normal); 3,330 tons (maximum)
Endurance: 6,310 miles at 10-12 knots

Complement
754

Fate(s)
Orion, scrapped from 1923.
Conqueror, scrapped from December 1923.
Monarch, used as a target, then deliberately sunk by *Revenge*, by searchlight, on 20 January 1925.
Thunderer, scrapped from April 1927.

Far left: The launch of the 'super dreadnought' *Orion* at Portsmouth on 20 August 1910. The information regarding this ship's armament led the general public to believe that she would be armed with an improved 12in gun on completion. Towards the end of 1911 the true facts were released regarding the considerable increase of bore to 13.5in. The turrets for these guns would be mounted along the centreline for the first time in a British dreadnought.

Below left: A view of *Orion*'s aft 13.5in turrets, with the island separating 'P' from the superimposed 'X' and 'Y' turrets. This photograph was taken in September 1911 when *Orion* was on preliminary sea trials. *Orion* belonged to the 1909 normal estimates, but her three sister-ships, *Thunderer, Conqueror* and *Monarch* were 'conditional dreadnoughts' authorized later under the same estimates. The normal 1909 programme included three battleships, *Colossus, Hercules* and *Orion*, and one battlecruiser (*Lion*) but, as only one battleship (*Neptune*) and one battlecruiser (*Indefatigable*) had been provided in the previous year and acceleration of new construction in Germany was anticipated, special provision was made in the 1909 estimates for laying down four more heavy ships should this be considered necessary. These comprised the three remaining *Orions* and the battlecruiser *Princess Royal*, all put in hand from April to May 1910.

Top right: *Orion* fitting out in Portsmouth Dockyard, 1912. Note the high freeboard of the vessel, which in turn gave the main armament a dry command. 13.5in turrets were positioned at 30ft 6in ('A'), 40ft ('B'), 24ft ('P'), 32ft 6in ('X') and 23ft ('Y').

Centre right: *Thunderer* on completion, showing her twin 13.5in turrets. *Thunderer* was the last big warship built on the River Thames. The builders, Thames Ironworks at Blackwall went into liquidation after the ship was completed in June 1912. *Thunderer* was commissioned at Devonport on 15 June 1912 and relieved the old predreadnought *Dominion* in the Home Fleet's 2nd Battle Squadron.

Below right: The fine lines of *Orion*, with funnel bands freshly painted in 1913. She was the 2nd Flagship of the 2nd Battle Squadron serving with the Home Fleet when this photograph was taken.

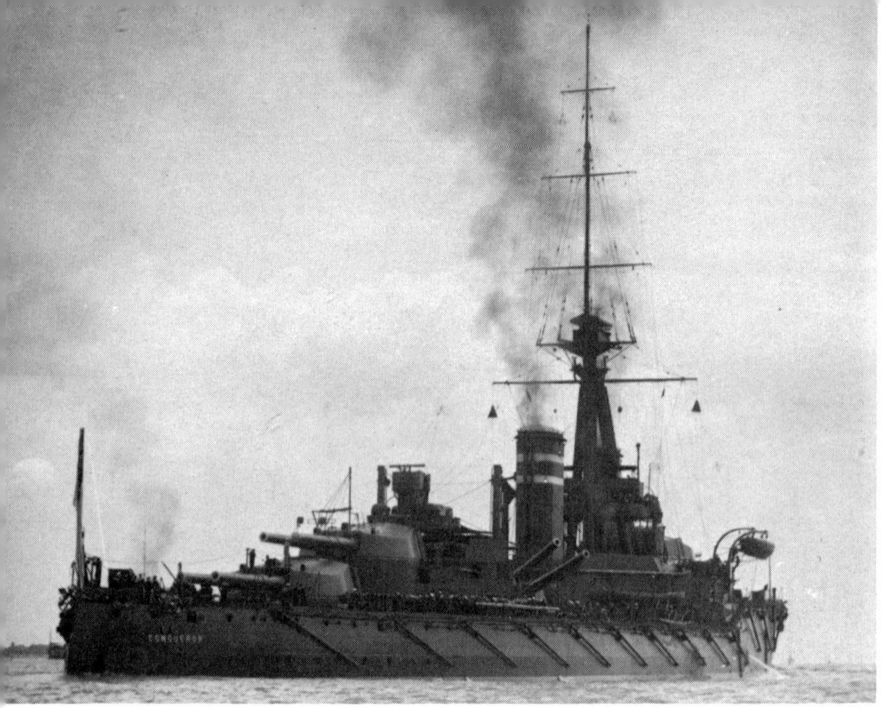

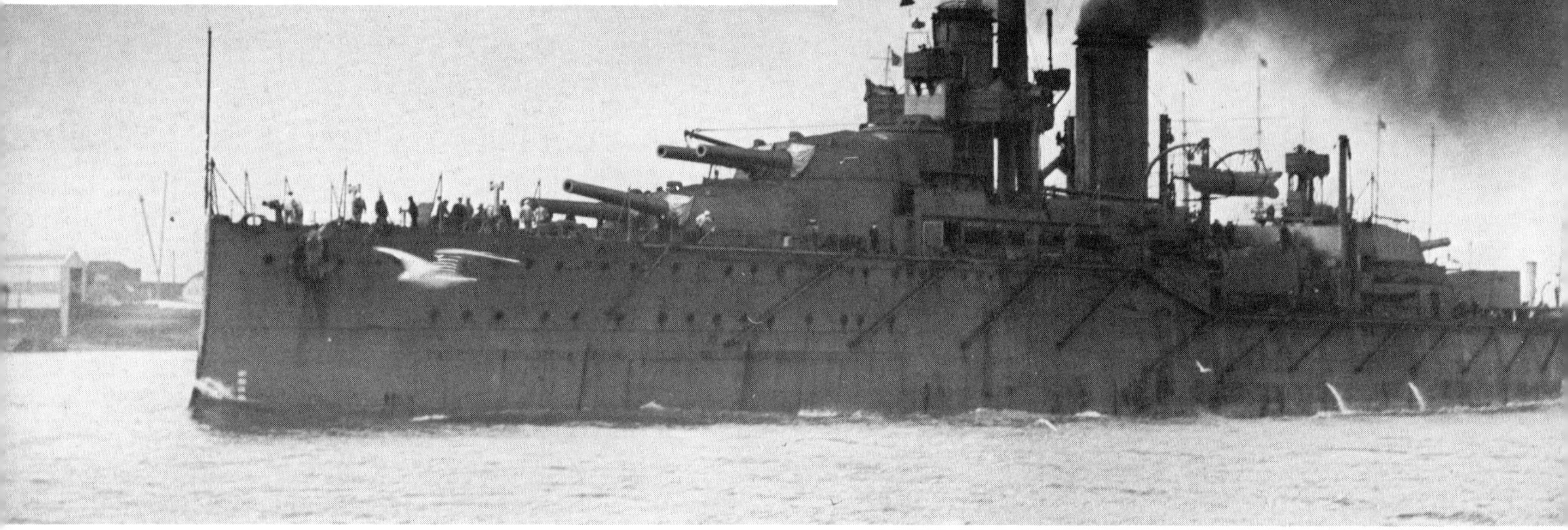

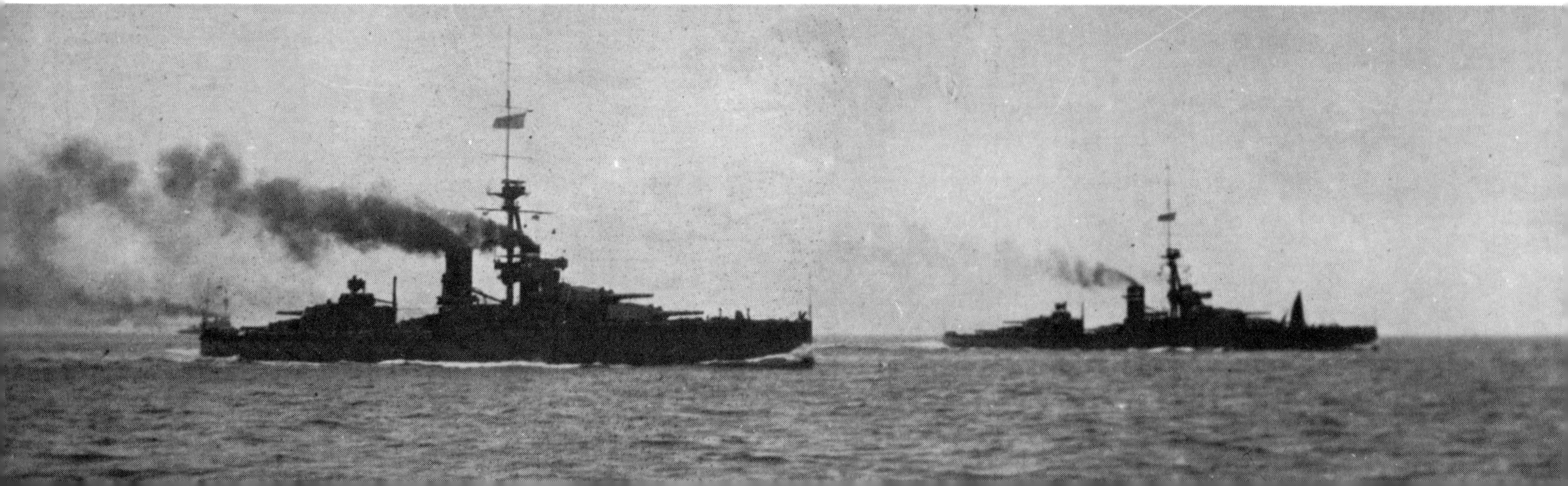

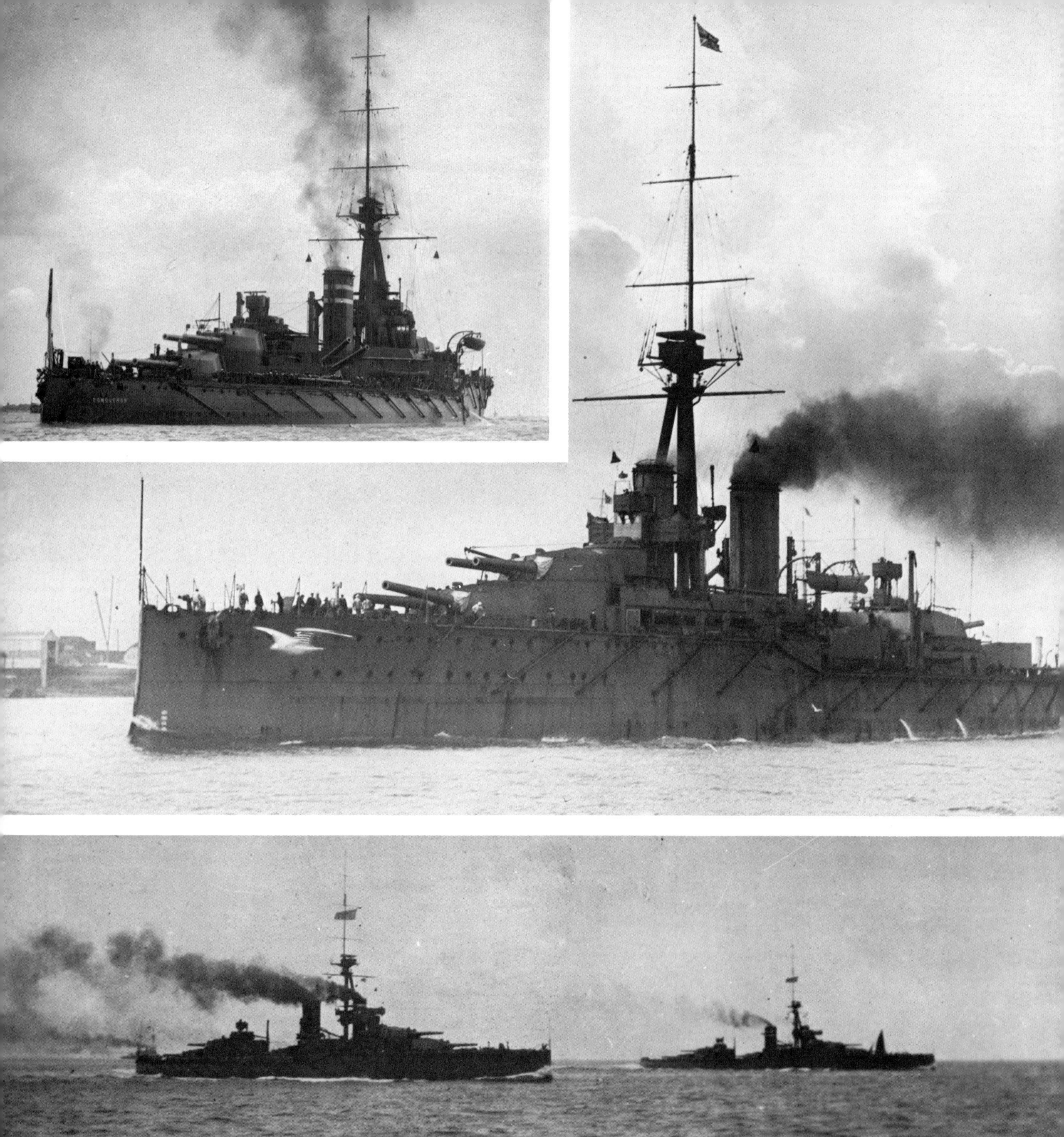

Far left: *Conqueror* showing her two white funnel bands on the aft funnel, 1913. *Thunderer* had three white bands on each funnel; *Orion*, two white on each funnel; and *Monarch*, two white on the forward funnel only.
Left: *Conqueror* on completion, leaving Portsmouth Harbour for her acceptance sea trials in November 1912. This photograph could be captioned 'The Two Fliers'. *Conqueror* is seen here 'flying' out of harbour at a fair speed, accompanied by a lone seagull heading the same way.
Below left: *Monarch* (foreground) at sea with her sister *Orion*, 1913/14. Both vessels were serving with the Home Fleet when the photograph was taken.
Right: *Monarch* in Swan Hunter's dry dock, having her hull and screws checked, 1912. The top view shows the plough bow to good advantage. The dry dock itself is worthy of mention: it had a displacement of 12,000 tons, a length of 680ft, the beam was 144ft and the lifting weight of the dock was claimed to be 32,000 tons. The accommodation quarters for the crew working on the ship were housed in the walls of the dock. Once a ship was in place, the pumps had to discharge nearly 46,000 tons of water to bring the vessel to working height.

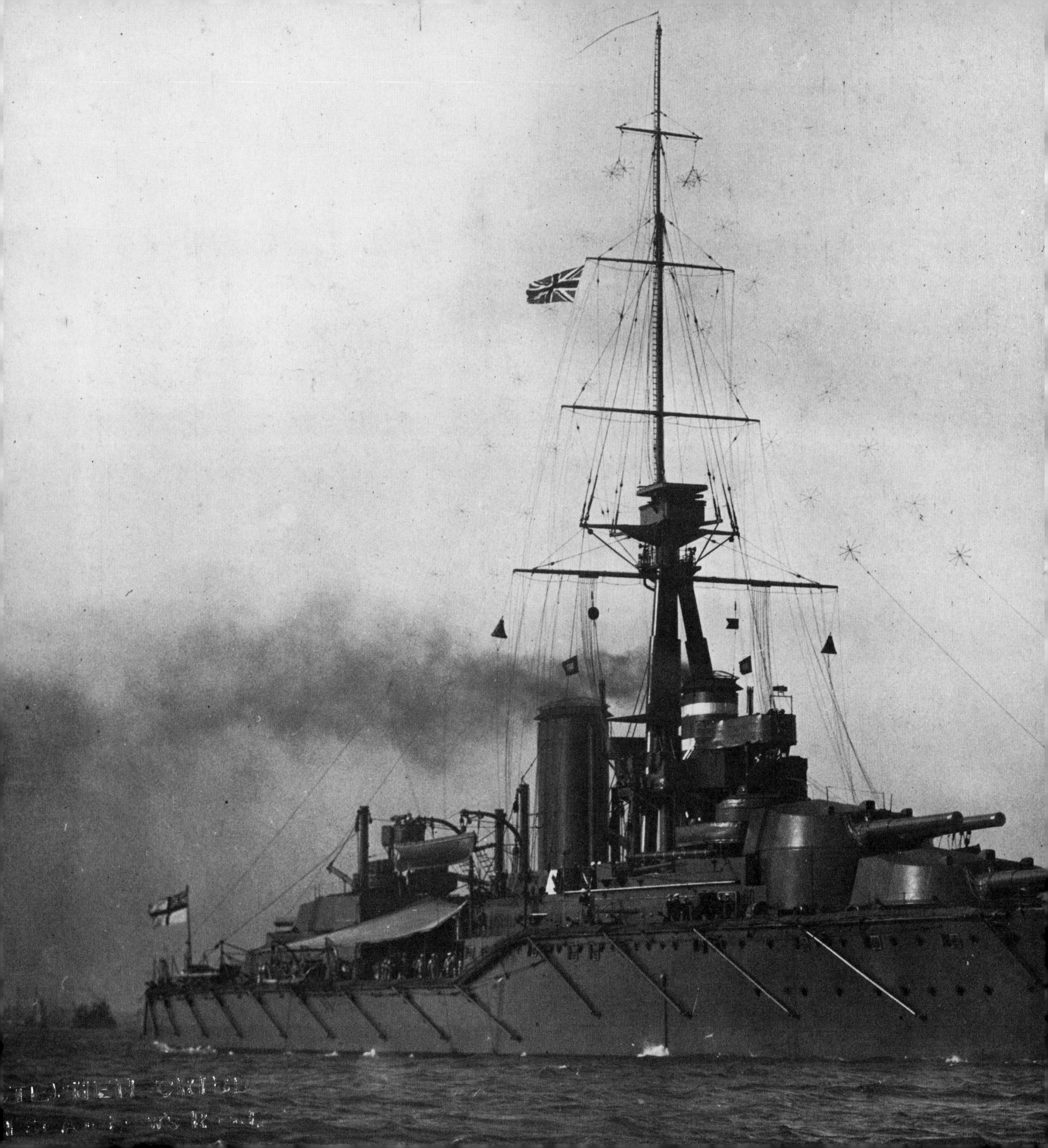

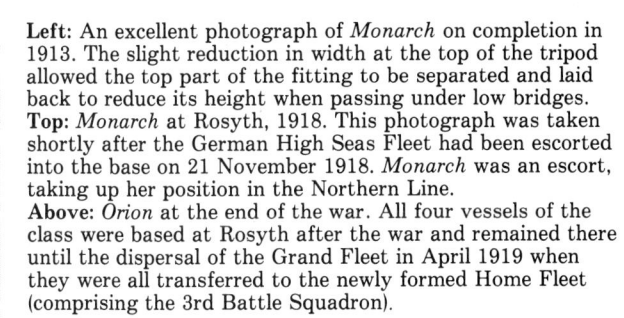

Left: An excellent photograph of *Monarch* on completion in 1913. The slight reduction in width at the top of the tripod allowed the top part of the fitting to be separated and laid back to reduce its height when passing under low bridges.
Top: *Monarch* at Rosyth, 1918. This photograph was taken shortly after the German High Seas Fleet had been escorted into the base on 21 November 1918. *Monarch* was an escort, taking up her position in the Northern Line.
Above: *Orion* at the end of the war. All four vessels of the class were based at Rosyth after the war and remained there until the dispersal of the Grand Fleet in April 1919 when they were all transferred to the newly formed Home Fleet (comprising the 3rd Battle Squadron).

41

Top: *Monarch* at war's end displaying all her modifications, 1919. These comprised bridge alterations, aircraft flying-off platforms on the turrets, searchlight towers around the aft funnel, an enlarged control top and director firing gear on the lower top and range clocks on the side of the control top.
Above: A port quarter shot of *Conqueror* at Rosyth shortly after the war, c.1918/19. It affords a good view of the after superstructure with the rangefinder fitted on top.
Top right: *Thunderer* entering Malta, 1923/24. From the end of 1921 until 1926, *Thunderer* was used as a sea-going training ship for cadets, and is seen here in that role.
Right: *Monarch* in service with the Mediterranean Fleet, early 1919. Note that each of the class differ in the arrangement of the aft superstructure, which carries the rangefinder and searchlights. The 4in secondary guns are now enclosed in casemates. *Monarch* carried only one aircraft runway on 'B' turret, unlike her sisters which were fitted with fore and aft mountings for aircraft.

43

LION CLASS

Name of ship:	*Lion*	*Princess Royal*	*Queen Mary*
Builder(s)	Devonport Royal Docks	Vickers Shipyard	Palmers Shipyard
Laid down:	29 November 1909	2 May 1910	6 March 1911
Launched:	6 August 1910	29 April 1911	20 March 1912
Completed:	May 1912	November 1912	September 1913

Displacement
Normal condition: 26,350 tons (excluding *Queen Mary*)
Deep load: 29,650 tons; 31,650 tons (*Queen Mary*)

Dimensions
Length: 660ft (waterline); 700ft (overall); 703ft (*Queen Mary*)
Beam: 88ft 6in; 89ft (*Queen Mary*)
Draught: 28ft 10in (normal); 31ft 4in (maximum)

Armament (as completed)
8-13.5in 45-calibre
16-4in
4-3pdr
5 machine-guns
4-21in tubes

Armour protection
Main belt: 9in
End belts: 6in-5in-4in
Bulkheads: 4in
Barbettes: 9in-8in-4in
Turrets: 9in-8in
Conning tower: 10in
Upper deck: 1in-1½in (*Queen Mary*, 2in)
Forecastle: 1¼in-1½in
Lower: 1½in
Magazine screens: 1½in-2½in

Machinery
Parsons direct-drive turbines with four screws
42 Yarrow large type boilers
70,000shp for speed of 26-27 knots

Fuel and endurance
1,000 tons of coal (normal); 3,520 tons (maximum)
Endurance: 5,610 miles at 10 knots

Complement
1,061-1,085

Fate(s)
Lion, scrapped from January 1924.
Princess Royal, scrapped from August 1923.
Queen Mary was lost at the Battle of Jutland on 31 May 1916. She came under fire from *Seydlitz* and *Derfflinger* and was sunk when her magazines blew up after hits to 'Q' turret and forward.

Above: *Lion*, famous for her wartime exploits, on surrender day, 21 November 1918. She is shown here with full wartime modifications. Her fine features are evident in this port broadside view, as is her unique funnel cap; *Lion* was the only battlecruiser to sport one of these fittings. Note the aircraft runways, with the fitting on 'Q' turret being of conventional design while that on 'Y' is extremely high and curved almost like a ski-slope.
Below: The mighty Battlecruiser Squadron passing the King, shortly after the end of the Fleet Review on 20 July 1914. Leading the line is one of the 'Splendid Cats', *Lion*, followed by her sister *Princess Royal* and half-sister *Queen Mary*, behind is *New Zealand*. The fleet dispersed after the review and made ready for war. The preparations were justified, with commencement of war being notified the following month.
Top right: A superb view of *Queen Mary* on completion, entering Portsmouth Harbour after her journey from Palmers Shipyard, May 1913. She was not fully worked-up until the following September, when she took her place alongside the 1st Battlecruiser Squadron. Her rounded centre funnel distinguished her from *Lion* and *Princess Royal*, both of which had flat-sided funnels. Note the high freeboard.
Below right: A port quarter view of *Queen Mary*, May 1913. This ship was completed with a single pole foremast, as can be seen in the previous photograph, but due to inadequate support for the top, in 1915 the vessel was given short support struts that formed a tripod.

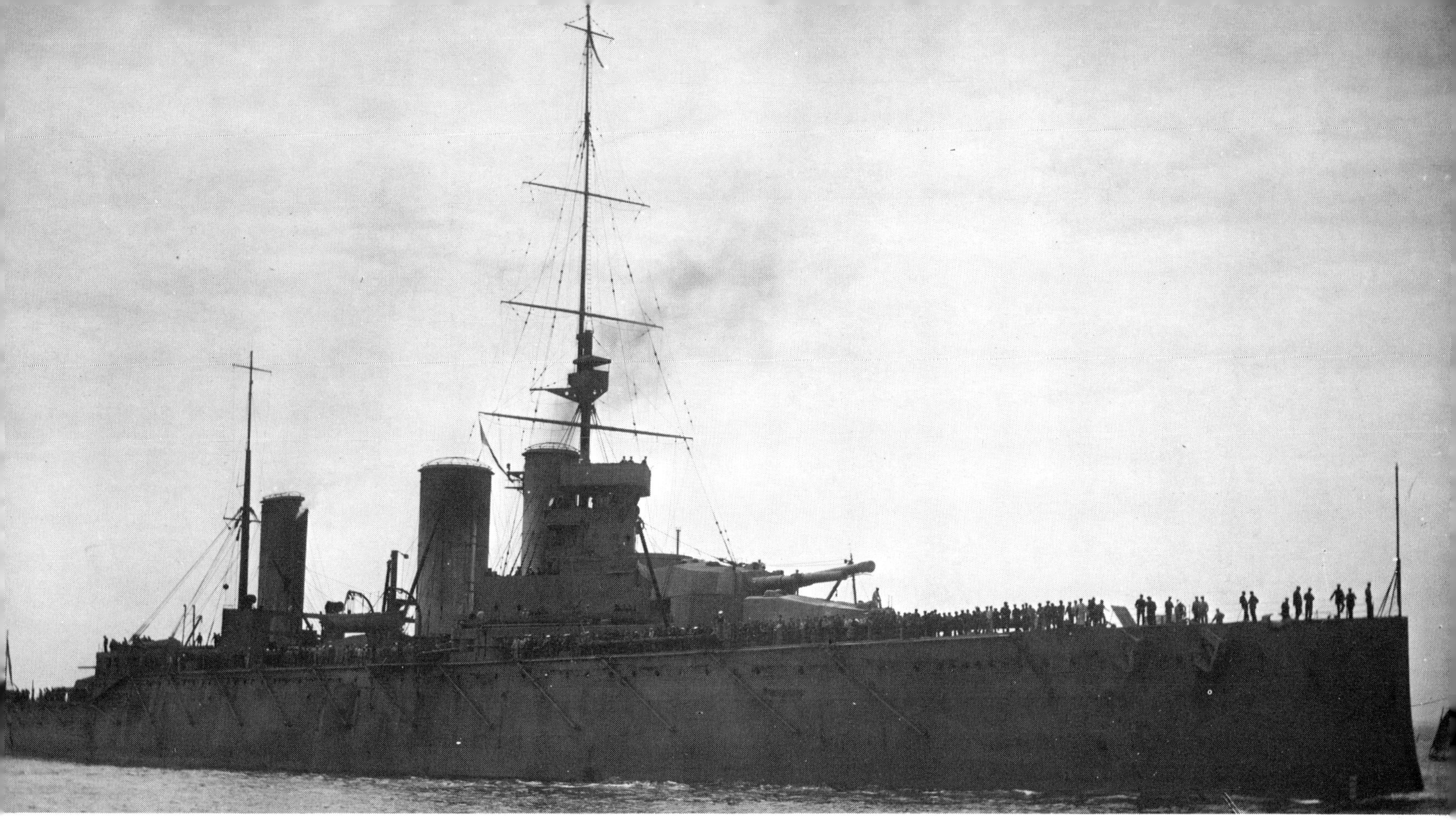
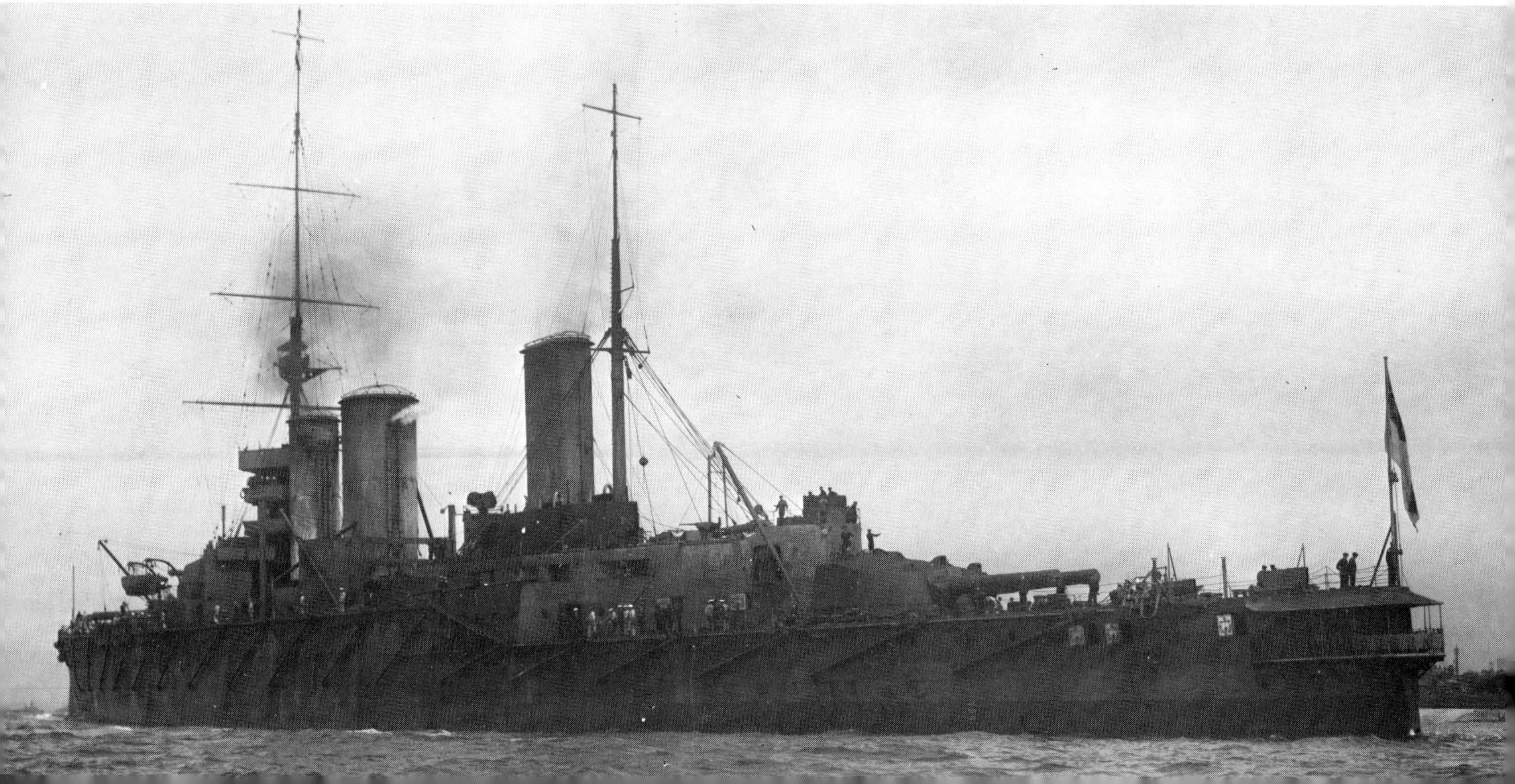

KING GEORGE V CLASS

Name of ship:	*King George V*	*Ajax*	*Centurion*	*Audacious*
Builder(s):	Portsmouth Royal Dockyard	Scotts Shipbuilding	Devonport Royal Dockyard	Cammell Laird Shipbuilders
Laid down:	16 January 1911	27 February 1911	16 January 1911	23 March 1911
Launched:	9 October 1911	21 March 1912	18 November 1911	14 September 1912
Completed:	October 1912	May 1913	February 1913	August 1913

Displacement
Normal condition: 23,000 tons
Deep load: 25,420 tons

Dimensions
Length: 589ft 6in (waterline); 597ft 9in (overall)
Beam: 89ft
Draught: 27ft (normal); 31ft (deep)

Armament (as completed)
10-13.5in 45-calibre
12-4in 50-calibre
1-12pdr (8cwt)
4-3pdr
5 machine-guns
10 Lewis guns
3-21in torpedo tubes

Armour protection
Main belt: 12in
End belts: 6in-4in-2½in
Bulkheads: 10in-8in-4in
Barbettes: 10in-9in-7in-6in
Turrets: 11in-4in-3in
Conning tower: 11in
Forecastle: 1in
Upper deck: 1½in-1¾in
Middle deck: 1in
Lower deck: 1in-2½in
Anti-torpedo protection: 1in-1¾in

Machinery
Parsons reduction turbines driving four screws
18 Babcock and Wilcox boilers (*King George V* and *Ajax*); Yarrow boilers (*Centurion* and *Audacious*)
27,000shp for a speed of 21 knots

Fuel and endurance
900 tons of coal (normal); 2,870 tons (maximum)
Endurance: 5,910 miles at 10 knots

Complement
869; 1,114 (wartime)

Fate(s)
King George V, scrapped from January 1927.
Ajax, scrapped from December 1926.
Centurion, sunk as breakwater off Verreville, Normandy, 9 June 1944.
Audacious, hit mine on 27 October 1914 and sank thirteen hours later.

Left, top: *Audacious* sporting funnel bands as painted up after commissioning on 21 October 1913. She joined the 2nd Battle Squadron of the Home Fleet on this date and remained so until the outbreak of war.

Left, below: *Ajax* shortly before leaving Portsmouth to start her first trials for the Royal Navy, April 1913. She had previously been commissioned at Portsmouth in March 1913 but, due to labour troubles at her builder's yard, was in an incomplete condition and returned to the yard after only several speed runs. She was completed to full capacity at Devonport. After her commissioning on 31 October 1913, she was placed in the 2nd Battle Squadron of the Home Fleet.

Below: *King George V* being launched at Portsmouth on 9 October 1911. The vessel was in a fairly advanced state of construction at launch, displacing 7,685 tons.

Right, top: A port quarter view of *Audacious* leaving for trials in September 1913. While on these trials she attained a speed of 22.1 knots with 29,300 shaft horsepower.

Right, below: *Audacious* undergoing her first sea trials in September 1913. Note the lack of anti-torpedo nets, a feature that was not uncommon for a vessel on early trials.

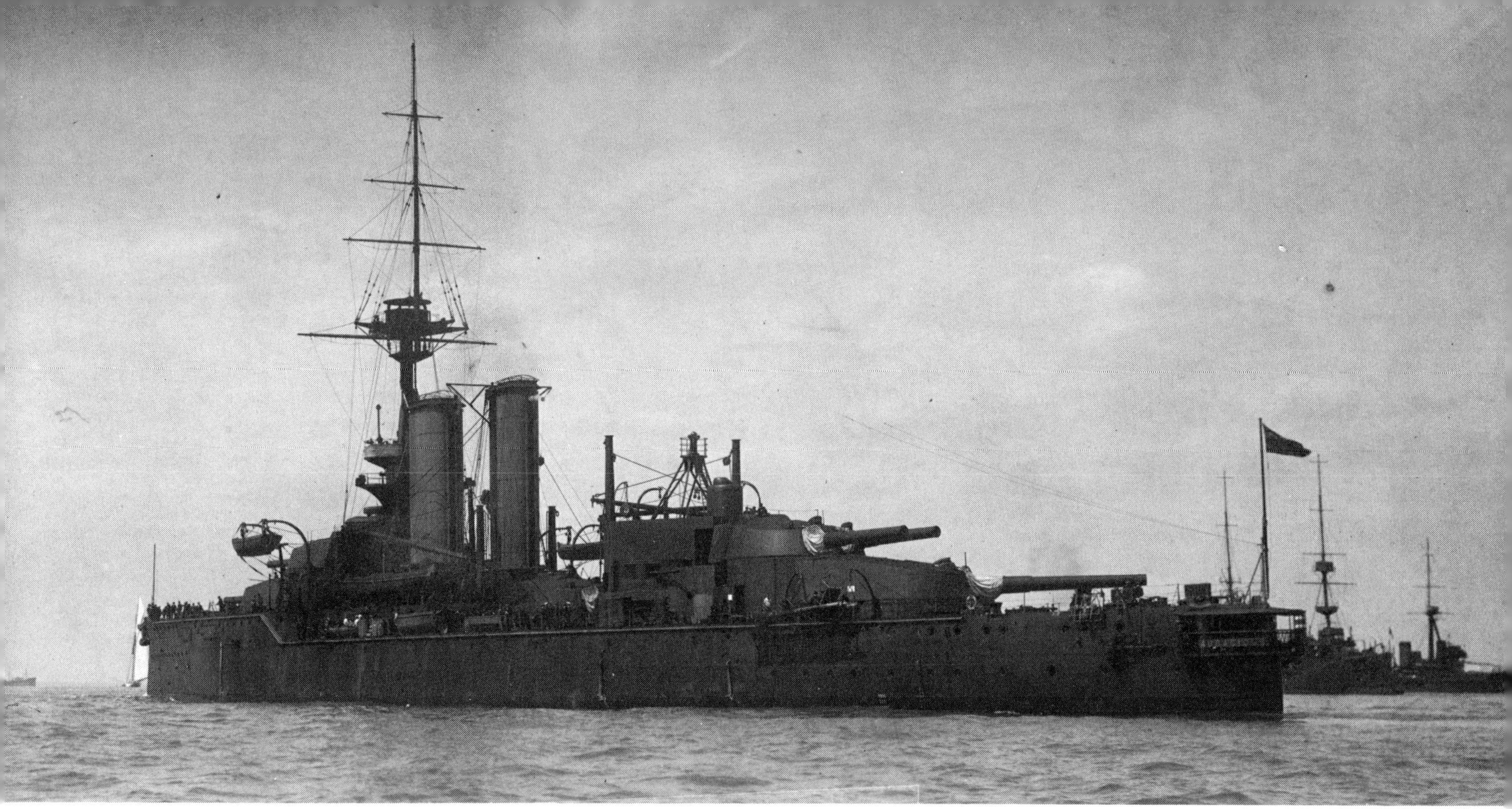

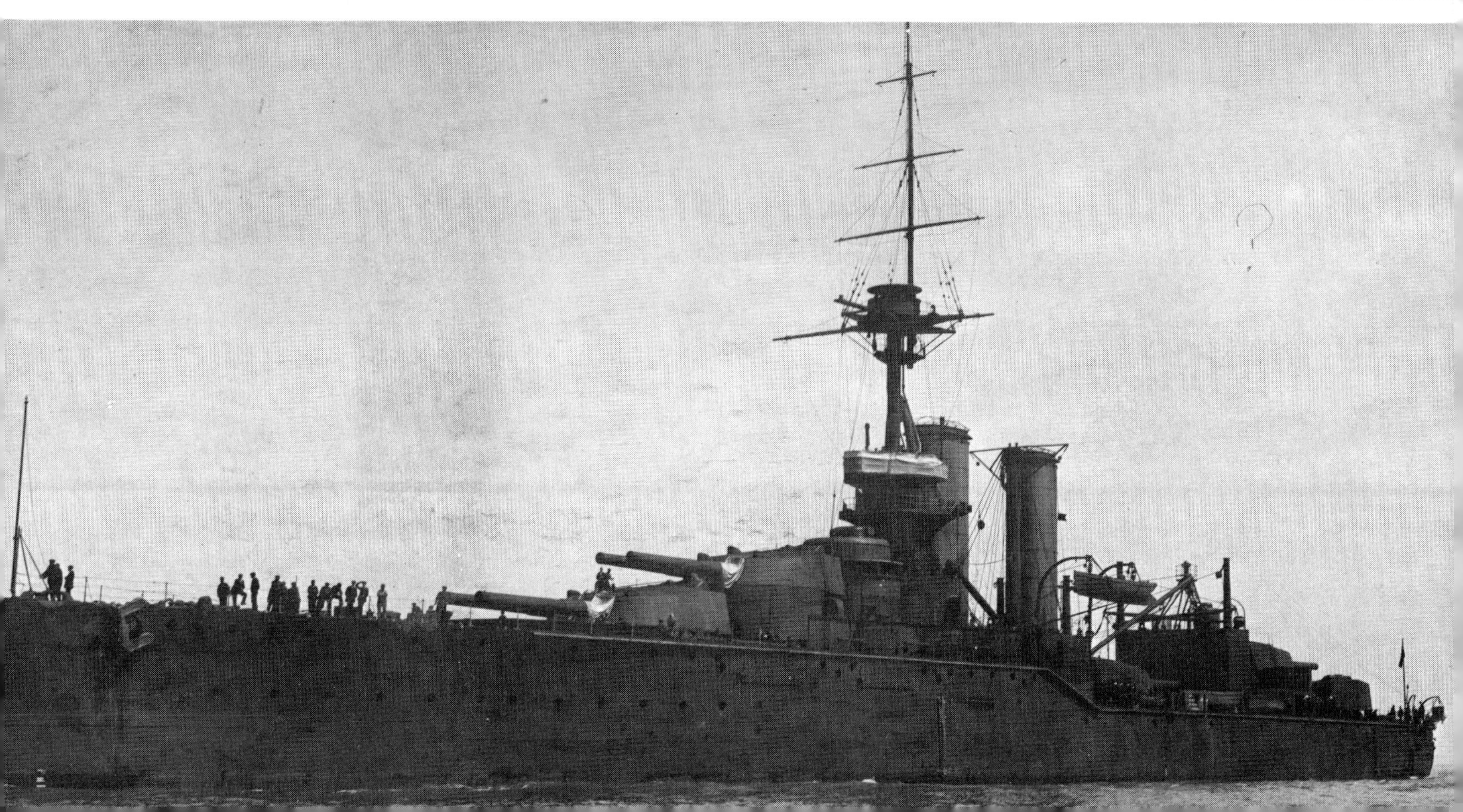

Top left: *King George V* at Kiel in 1914. She and her three sisters were paying a friendly visit to the port, where they were much admired by German naval officers who expressed great interest in the vessels' design and layout.
Centre left: *King George V* as commissioned in November, 1912. She is seen here at Weymouth, acting as Flagship of the 2nd Battle Squadron of the Home Fleet. Note the single pole foremast with supporting girders attached. This was the first in a series of experiments to investigate which type of support would be best to ensure a steady foretop free from vibration. Unfortunately, it proved a failure and, after much debate, the vessel ended up with complete support legs similar to the original tripod of previous battleship designs.
Below left: *Centurion* in 1914, showing the director control gear for the main armament on the foretop. The foremasts differed in all ships of the class. *Centurion* was completed with a single pole mast, as in *King George V*, but after early trials she was fitted with stays, which supported the pole and gave a vibration-free control top. The legs of the stays terminated just below the lower platform, which was sufficient for a steadfast position and easier to fit than stays extending to the foretop.
Top right: *King George V* as completed in November 1912. This photograph shows the old and the new very well, with the new *King George V* flanked by the *Victory* of 1765 (to the right) and a unit of the *Majestic* class from 1894 (on the left).
Centre right: *King George V* in October 1912 undergoing her trials. Note that the rangefinder has not yet been fitted to the conning tower.
Below right: *King George V* leaving Rosyth shortly before the cessation of war in 1918. Even with her wartime addditions and improvements, the ship's basic appearance remains unaltered.

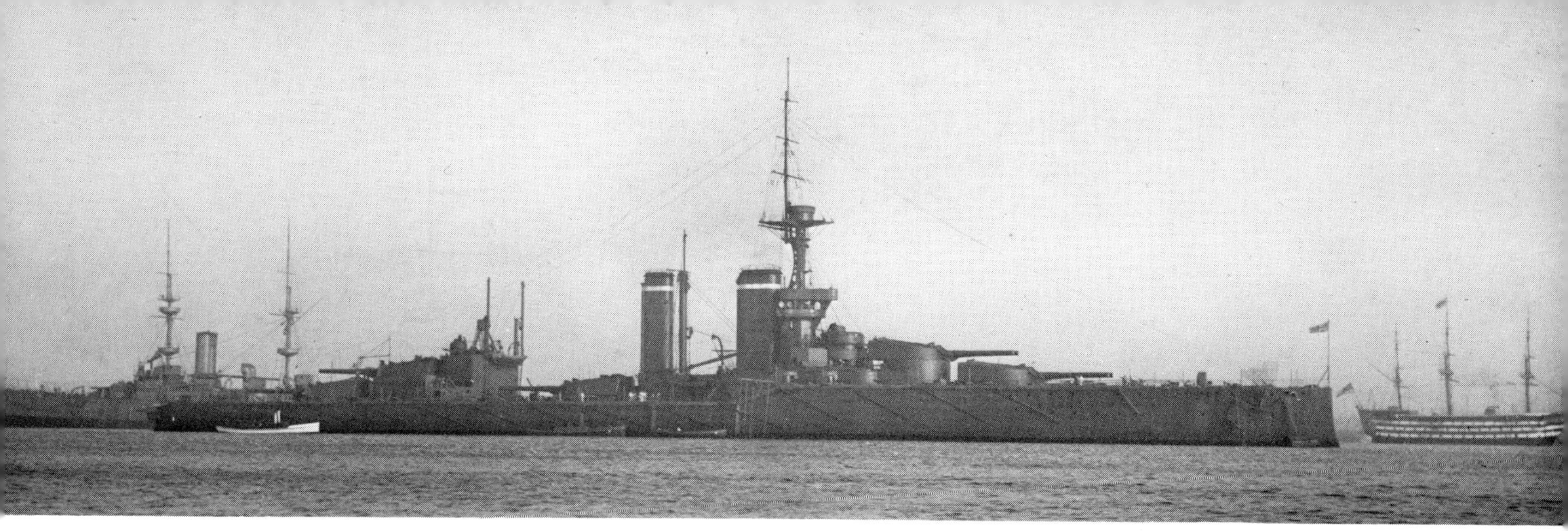

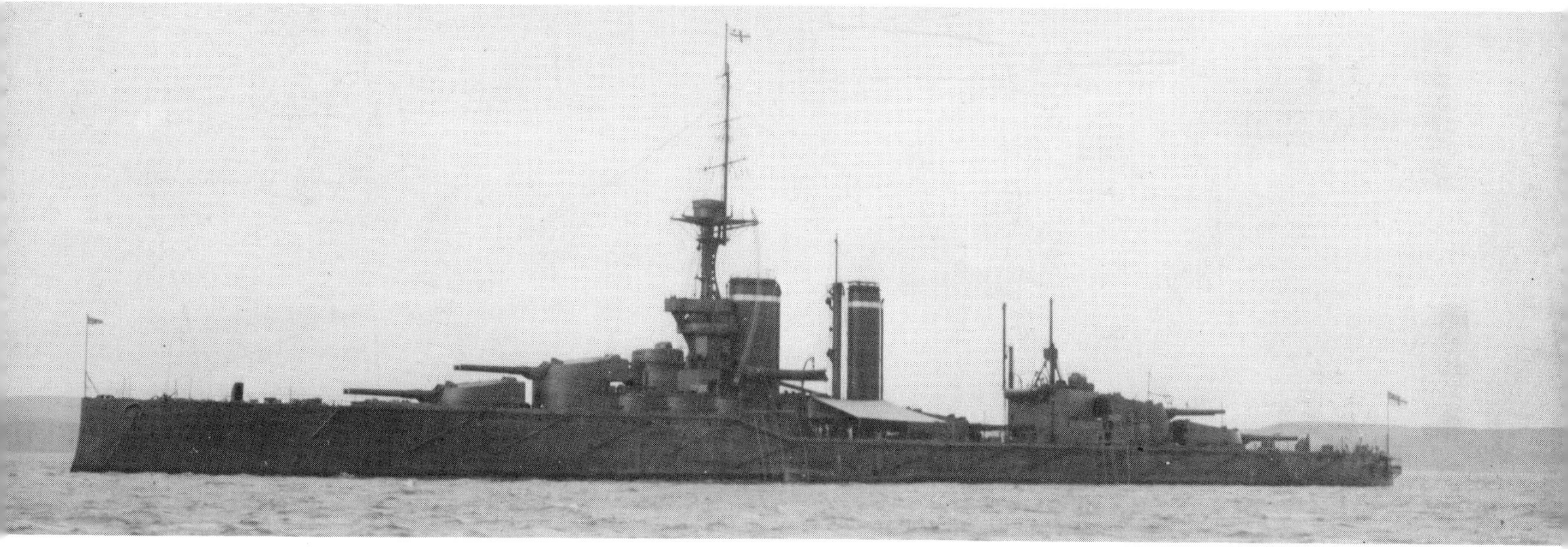

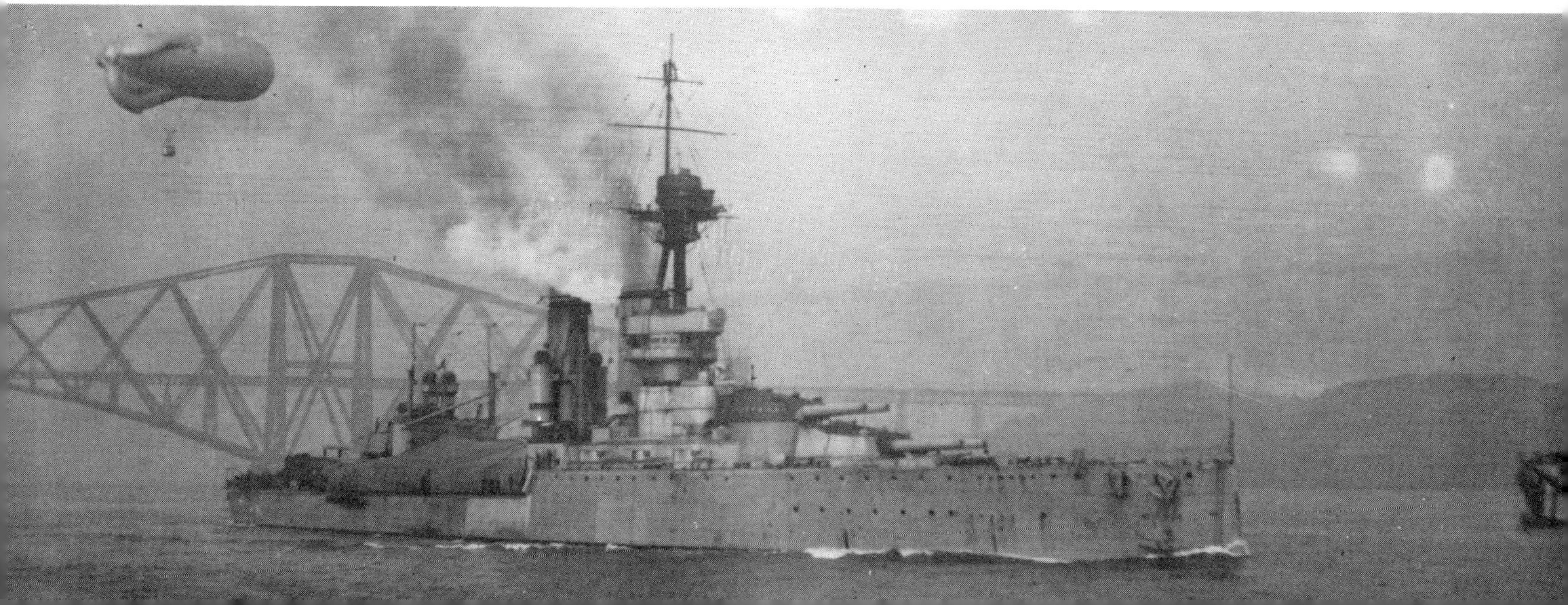

Left: *Ajax* in 1921, showing her rather majestic profile with the heavy bridgework on the foremast and large control top. She was serving as a unit of the 4th Battle Squadron in the Mediterranean when this photograph was taken.
Below: *Centurion* entering Valetta Harbour in the early twenties. Note the rangefinder clocks and searchlight layout, which was slightly different in the three surviving ships of the class. All three were easily identified from each other by their bridge differences and searchlight tower arrangements. Although excellent battleships, the ships of this class were not regarded as highly as they might have been, purely because of their insufficient secondary battery.

Top right: *Centurion* fitted in her role as a radio-controlled target ship, 1930/31. The actual conversion took place at Chatham from 20 April 1926 until 27 July 1927, when all armament, small fittings, control top and searchlights were removed. She replaced the old predreadnought *Agamemnon* after completion of this refit. During her years as a target ship, *Centurion's* appearance did not remain unchanged. In the mid 1930s, the height of her funnels was reduced, giving the ship a rather bizarre profile.
Below right: *Centurion* as a radio-controlled target ship, 1936. Her superstructure and funnels have been reduced, and some of her barbettes have been removed.

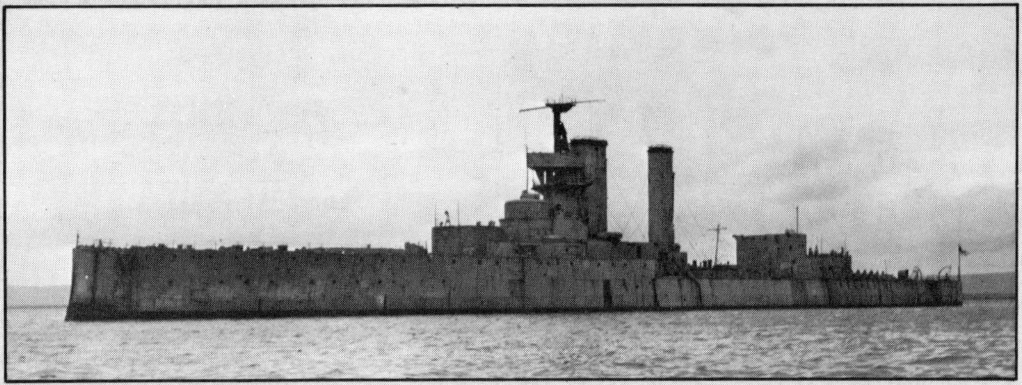
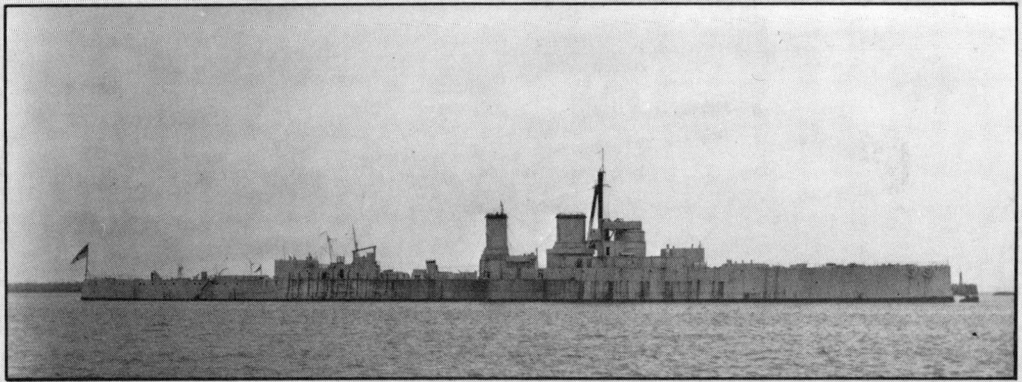
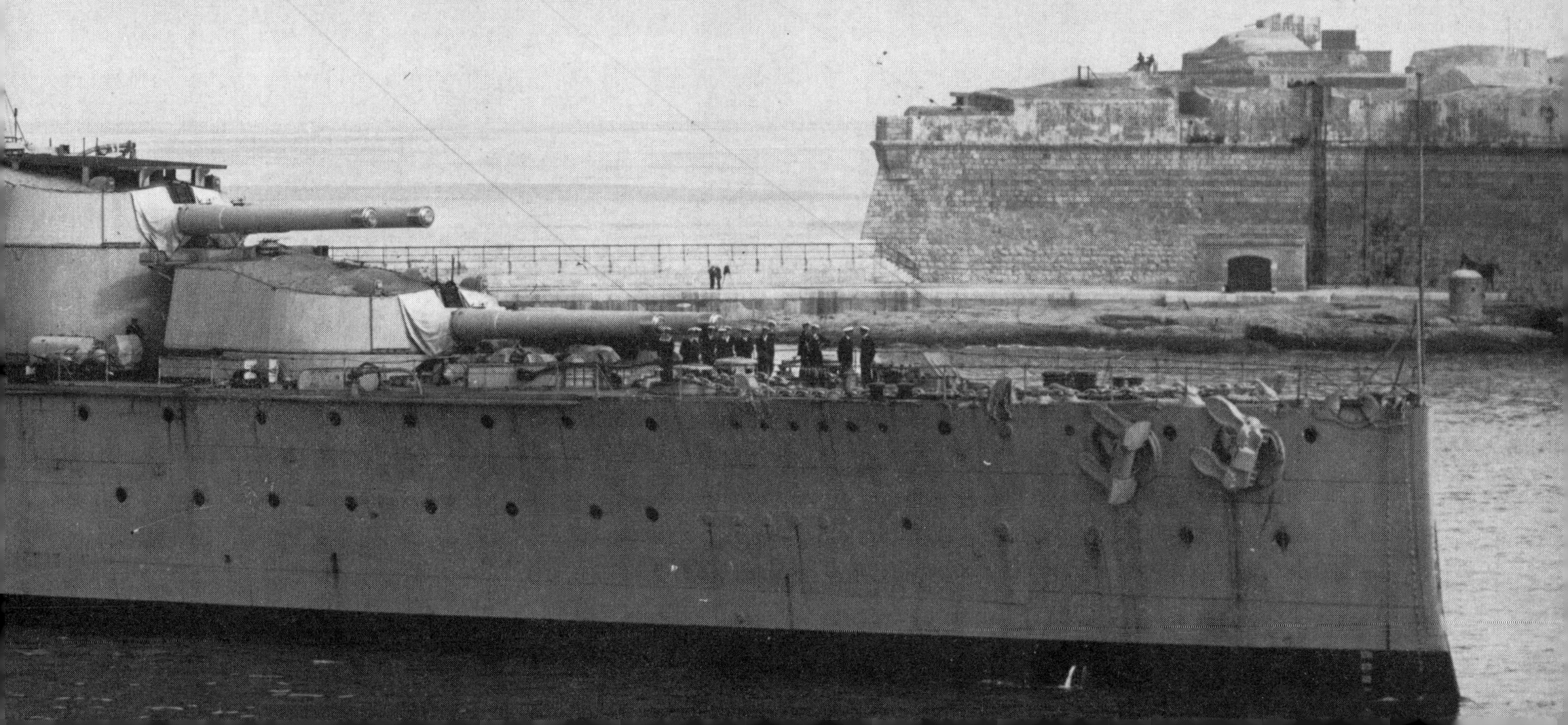

IRON DUKE CLASS

Name of ship:	*Iron Duke*	*Marlborough*	*Benbow*	*Emperor of India*
Builder(s):	Portsmouth Royal Dockyard	Devonport Royal Dockyard	Beardmore Shipbuilding	Vickers Shipbuilding
Laid down:	15 January 1912	25 January 1912	30 May 1912	31 May 1912
Launched:	12 October 1912	24 October 1912	12 November 1913	27 November 1913
Completed:	March 1914	March 1914	October 1914	October 1914

Displacement
Normal condition: 25,000 tons (designed); 26,100 (actual)
Deep load: 31,400 tons

Dimensions
Length: 614ft 3in (waterline); 623ft 9in (overall)
Beam: 90ft 1in
Draught: 28ft 8in (normal); 32ft 9in (deep)

Armament (as completed)
10-13.5in 45-calibre
12-6in
1-12pdr (8cwt) field-gun
4-3pdr
5 machine-guns
10 Lewis guns
4-21in torpedo tubes

Armour protection
Main belt: 12in
Upper belt: 8in
End belts: 6in-4in
Bulkheads: 8in-6in
Barbettes: 10in-9in-8in-4in
Turrets: 11in
Conning tower: 11in
Forecastle: 1in
Upper deck: 1¼in-2in
Main deck: 1½in
Middle deck: 1½in-2½in
Lower deck: 1in-2½in
Anti-torpedo protection: 1in-1½in

Machinery
Parsons direct-drive turbines with four screws (reaction type)
18 Yarrow boilers (*Marlborough* and *Emperor of India*); 18 Babcock and Wilcox boilers (*Iron Duke* and *Benbow*)
29,000shp for a speed of 21.25 knots

Fuel and endurance
900 tons of coal (normal); 3,250 tons (maximum)
Endurance: 8,100 miles at 12 knots

Complement
925-1,102

Fate(s)
Iron Duke, scrapped from September 1948.
Marlborough, scrapped from June 1932.
Benbow, scrapped from April 1931.
Emperor of India, scrapped from February 1932 after being used as a target.

Top: The launch of *Iron Duke* at Portsmouth, October 1912. Note the recesses in the vessel's sides showing the position for the armoured plates, which were to be fitted at a later date.
Below: *Iron Duke* on sea trials in the summer of 1914. Note the small plates over the 6in gun ports; this feature did not prove successful because the plates had to be dropped before the gun could be brought to action. They were removed before 1915. The vessel was fitted with anti-torpedo nets while on builders preliminary trials, but these were removed on commissioning, before carrying out her Royal Navy trials.
Top right: *Marlborough* on completion, 1914. She was almost identical with *Iron Duke* except for a small rangefinder placed over the bridge in the latter (1914 only, removed later).
Below right: *Emperor of India* on listing trials in 1918. All battleships underwent such trials upon completion, although in some cases a lengthy programme was not possible owing to wartime conditions. Towards the end of the war, however, it was a frequent sight to see vessels in this inclining condition in Scapa Flow, where it was now thought to be safe from any enemy interference.
Far right, below: A very wet forecastle indeed: *Marlborough* in a heavy swell off Torbay on 9 July 1929. The aircraft platform is still fitted to the top of 'B' turret.

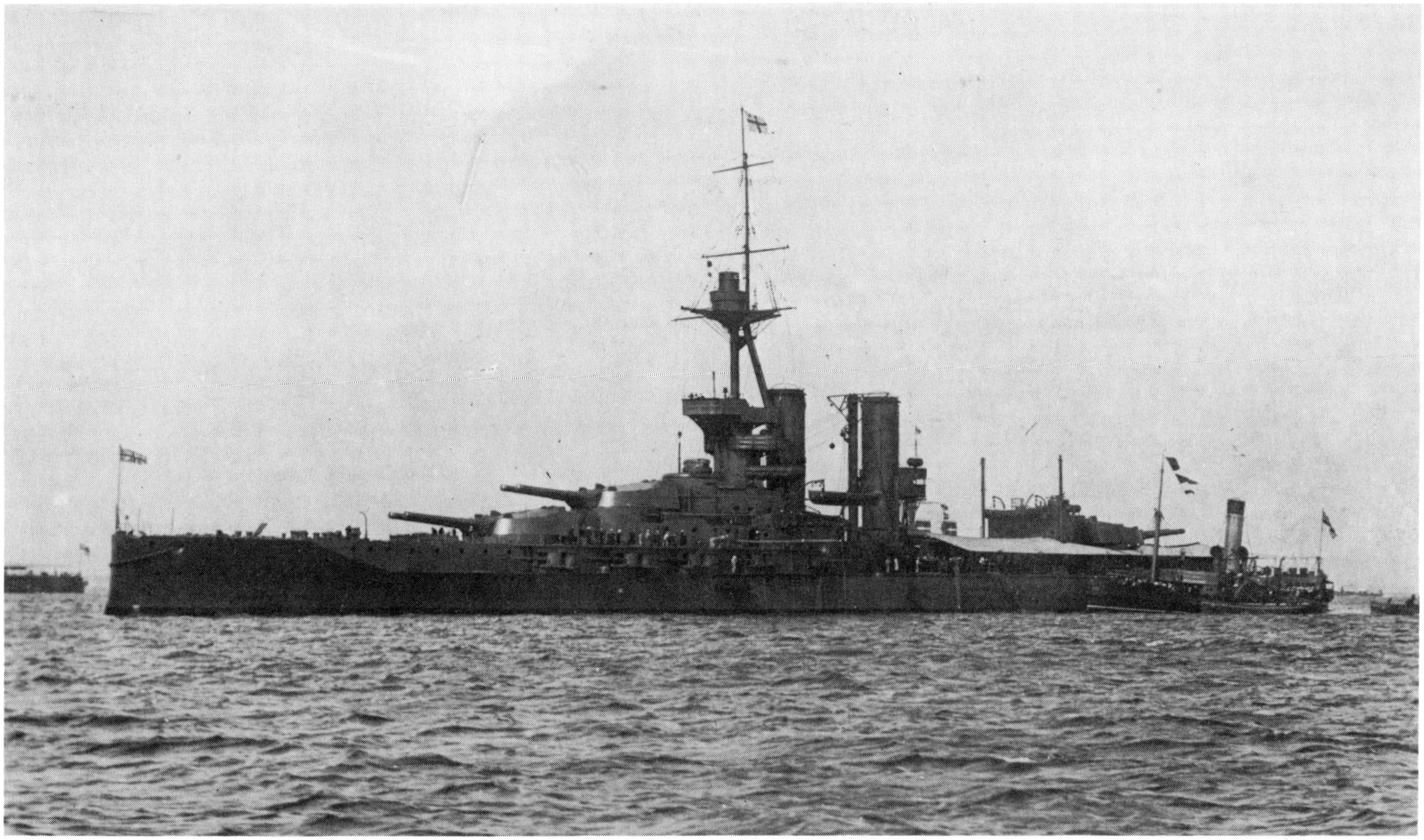

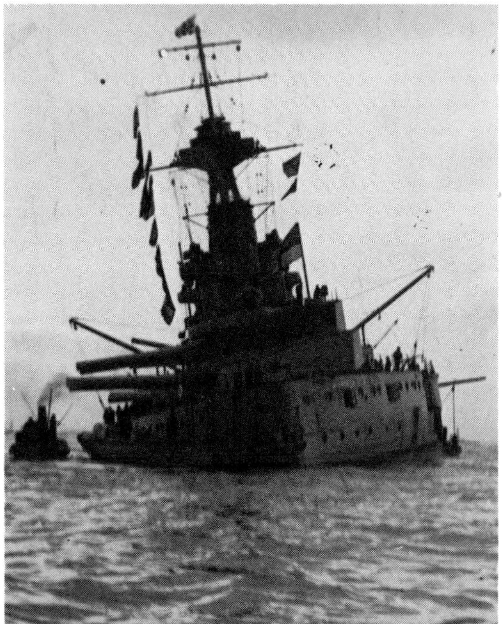

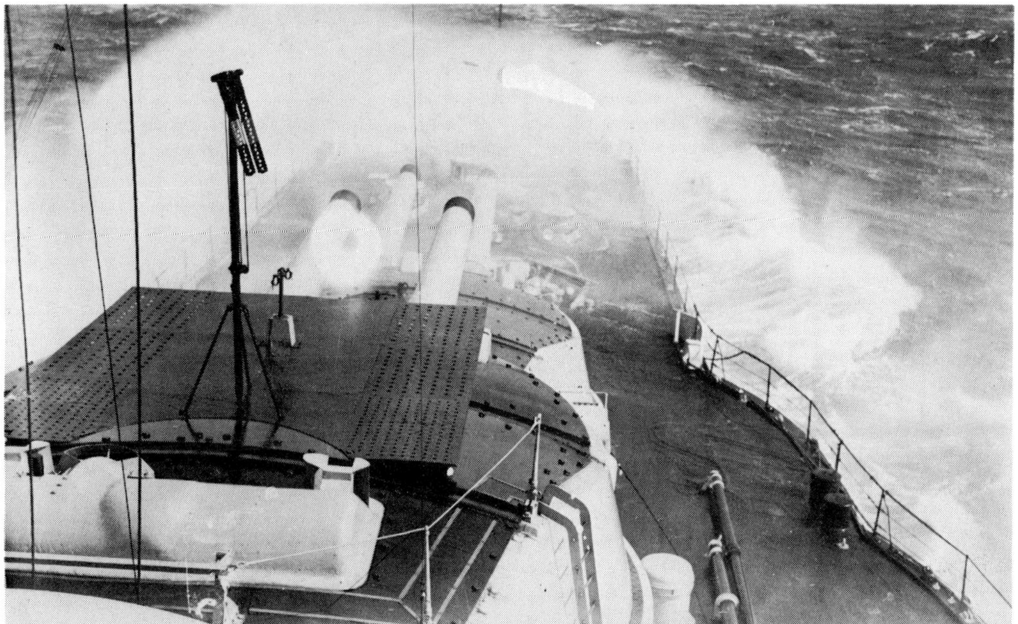

Left and below: Two superb shots of *Emperor of India* in 1918, enabling a clear view of her aft arrangement and her bridge and foremast details. *Emperor of India* was the only unit of the class to have a cap fitted to the fore funnel. Note the kite balloon being towed by the ship for observation experiments.
Top right: *Benbow* with *Iron Duke* in the background, 1924/25. Both vessels were units of the 4th Battle Squadron with the Mediterranean Fleet, *Iron Duke* being the Flagship of the Commander-in-Chief. Note the heavy bridges.
Below right: A head-on view of *Iron Duke*, c.1925, showing her forecastle, bridge and anchor arrangements. Note the large control top, which also housed the director control equipment.
Far right, below: A rest period on board *Iron Duke* after the war, showing the clean lines of the forecastle deck with many tired bodies sprawled around soaking up an afternoon's sunshine, a welcome period for 'Jack' at sea. The aircraft runway on 'B' turret suggests a date of 1926/27. *Iron Duke* was demilitarized in 1931/32 and served for many years as a Seagoing Gunnery Training ship. She was finally scrapped in 1946.

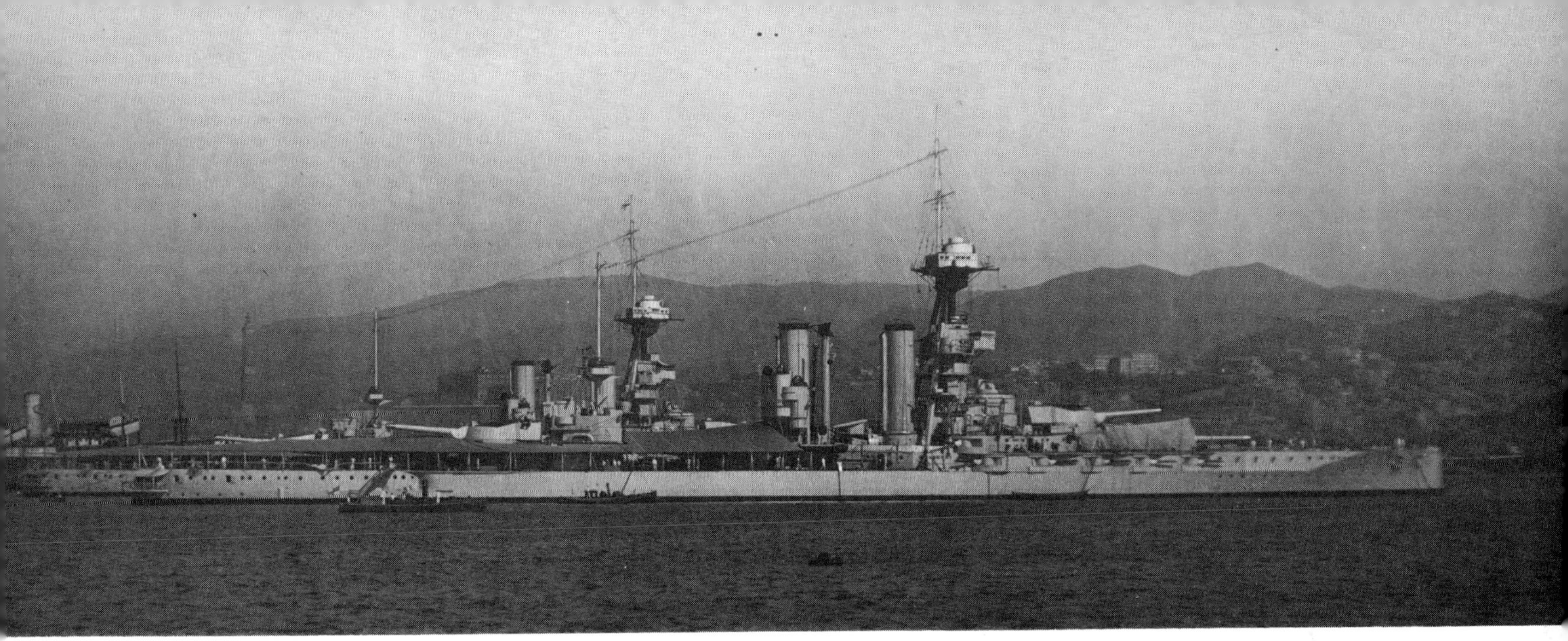

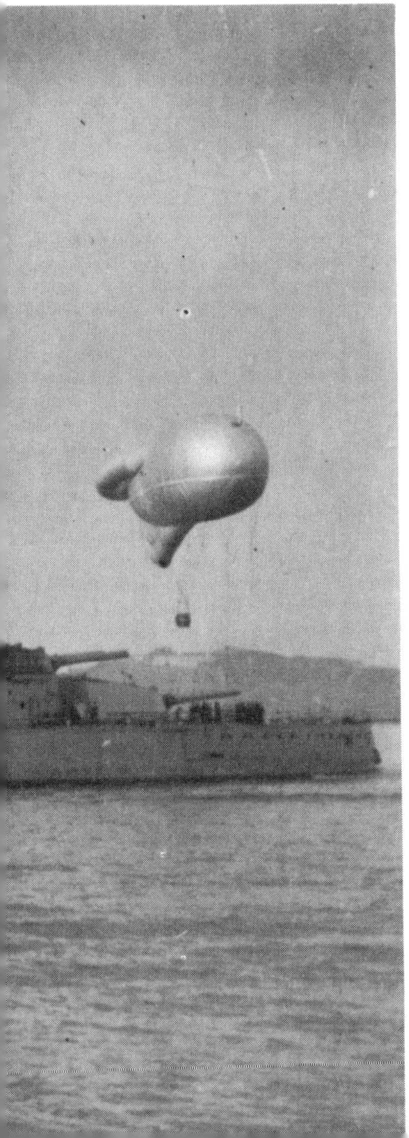

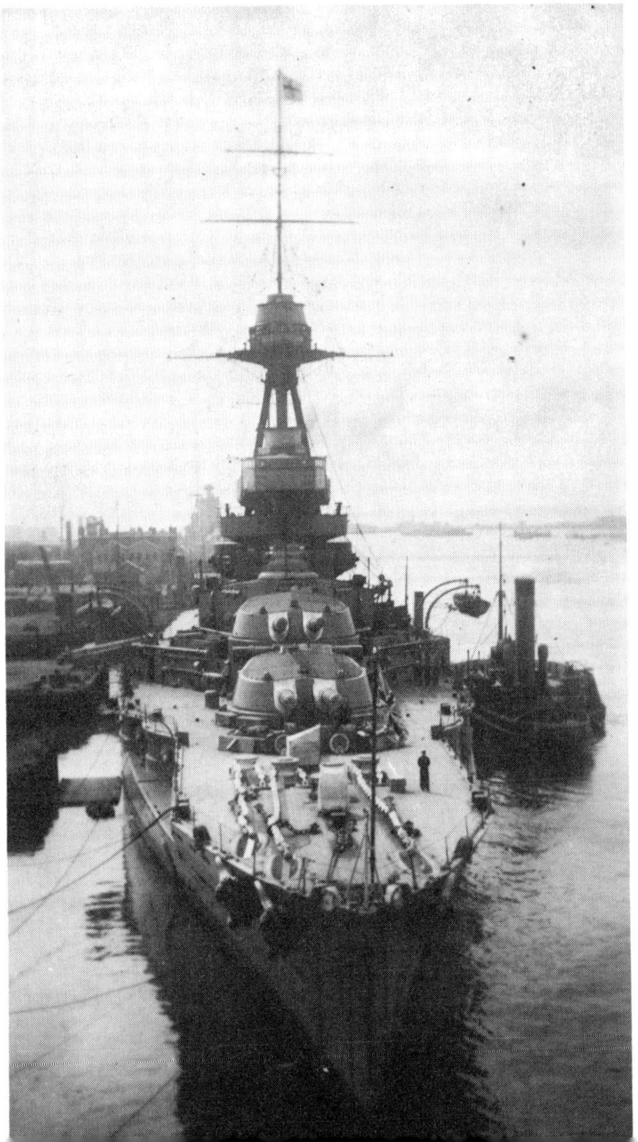

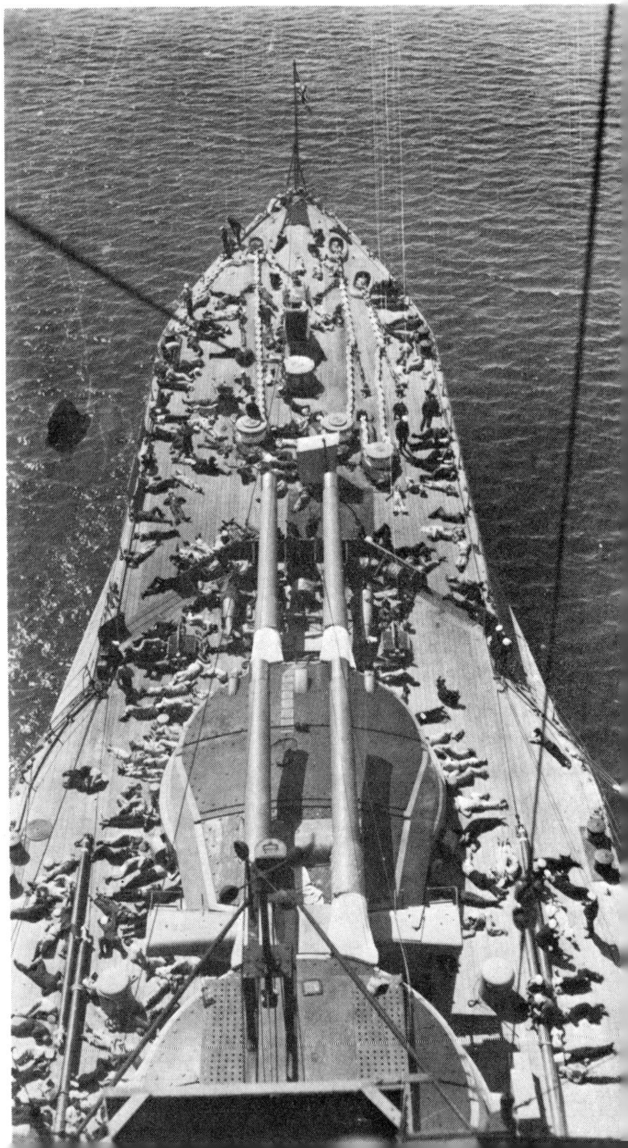

TIGER

Builder(s): John Brown Shipyard
Laid down: 20 June 1912
Launched: 15 December 1913
Completed: 3 October 1914

Displacement
Normal condition: 29,560 tons
Deep load: 33,220 tons

Dimensions
Length: 660ft (between perpendiculars); 704ft (overall)
Beam: 90ft 6in
Draught: 29ft 4in (normal); 32ft 4in (deep)

Armament (as completed)
8-13.5in 45-calibre
12-6in 45-calibre
4-3pdr
1-12pdr (8cwt)
5 machine-guns
4-21in torpedo tubes

Armour protection
Main belt: 9in
End belts: 5in-4in-3in
Bulkheads: 5in-4in
Barbettes: 9in-8in-4in
Turrets: 9in
Conning tower: 10in
Forecastle: 1½in
Upper deck: 1in
Main deck: 1in
Lower deck: 1in-3in
Magazine screens: 1½in-2½in

Machinery
Brown and Curtis direct-drive turbines with four screws
39 Babcock and Wilcox boilers
108,000shp for a speed of 29 knots

Fuel and endurance
450 tons of oil/coal (minimum); 3,320 tons of coal (maximum), 3,480 tons of oil (maximum)
Endurance: 5,700 miles at 12 knots, 5,200 miles at 15 knots and 2,800 miles at 25 knots

Complement
1,185-1,434

Fate(s)
Tiger was scrapped under the Washington Treaty's Age Clause and towed to Inverkeithing after being dismantled at Rosyth in March 1932.

Note
She was considered to be the finest looking ship to be found in any navy.

Below: *Tiger* as completed, August 1914. She is seen here after leaving John Brown's Shipyard, making her way down the Clyde to prepare for her preliminary sea trials. This broadside photograph shows to advantage her beautiful lines and marked flare at the bows. She was to gain a reputation as the best-looking warship of her day, with none able to match the perfect balance of her design. She is seen here in the light condition, and would probably have carried enough fuel to complete the speed runs that were required to ascertain her maximum speed. Her funnels are round in shape and not flat as in previous battle-cruisers.

Right: *Tiger* in September 1921, showing her modifications. With the fitting of a topmost on the derrick stump, she seems to have lost her balanced appearance, although the increased bridge structure and heavier foretop do make her look more formidable. Aircraft runways can be seen on 'B' and 'Q' turrets, and the vessel has new searchlight towers at the base of the third funnel.

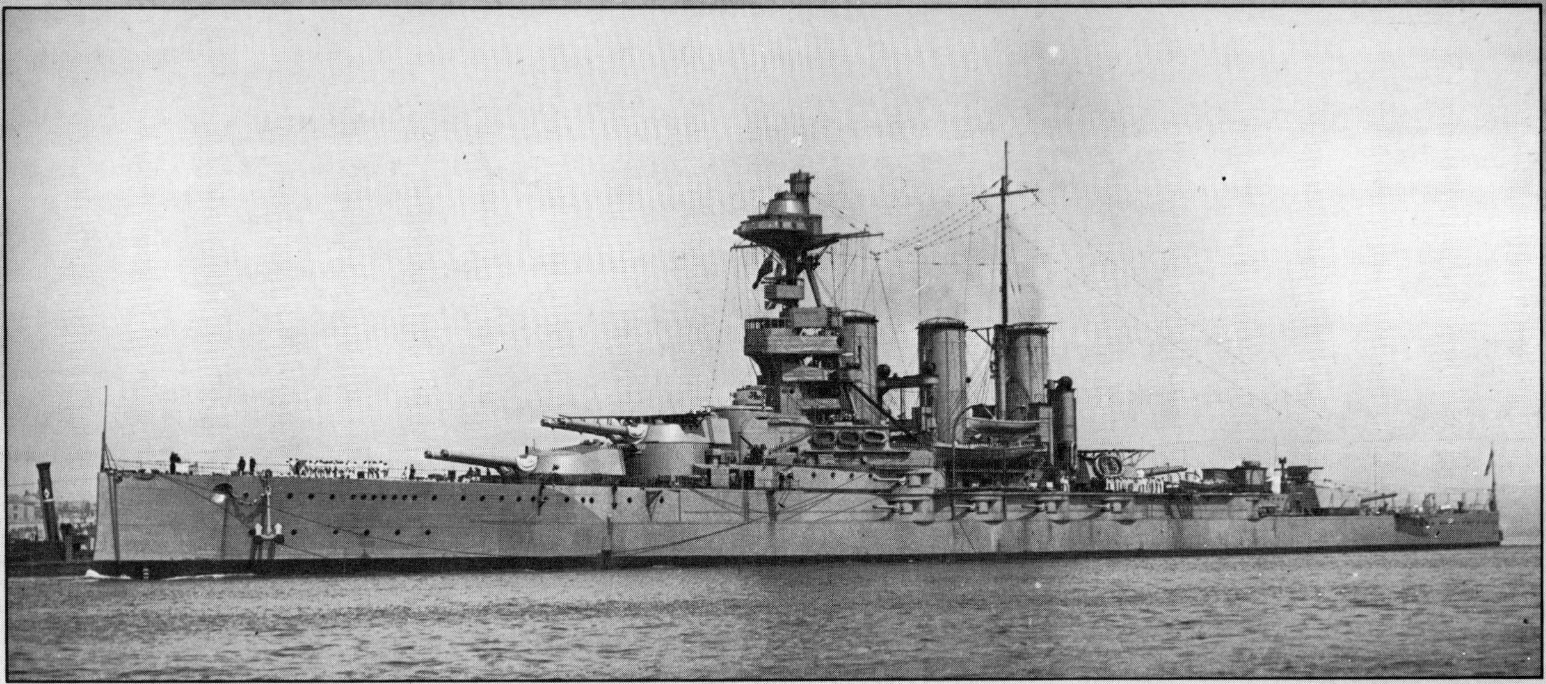

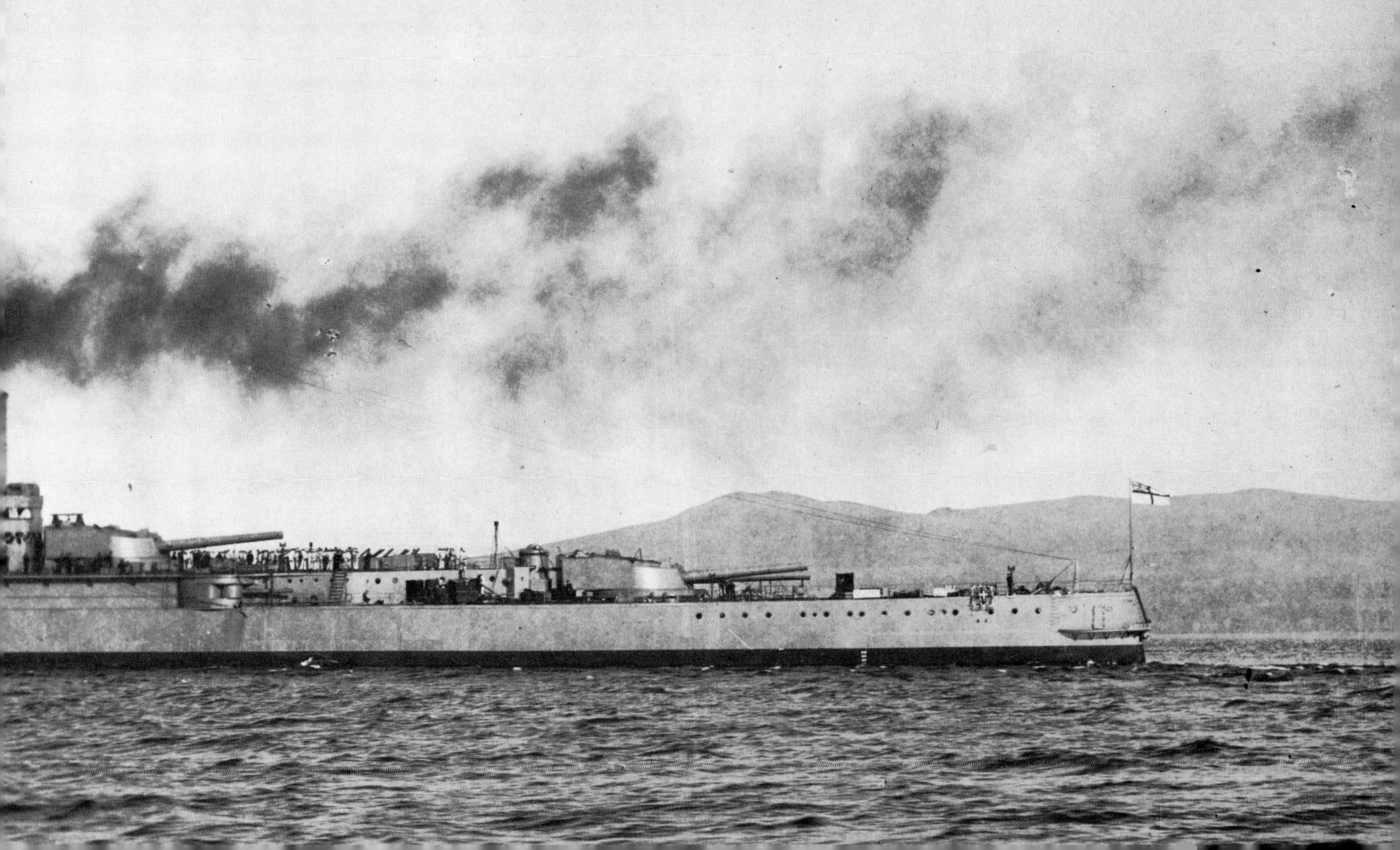

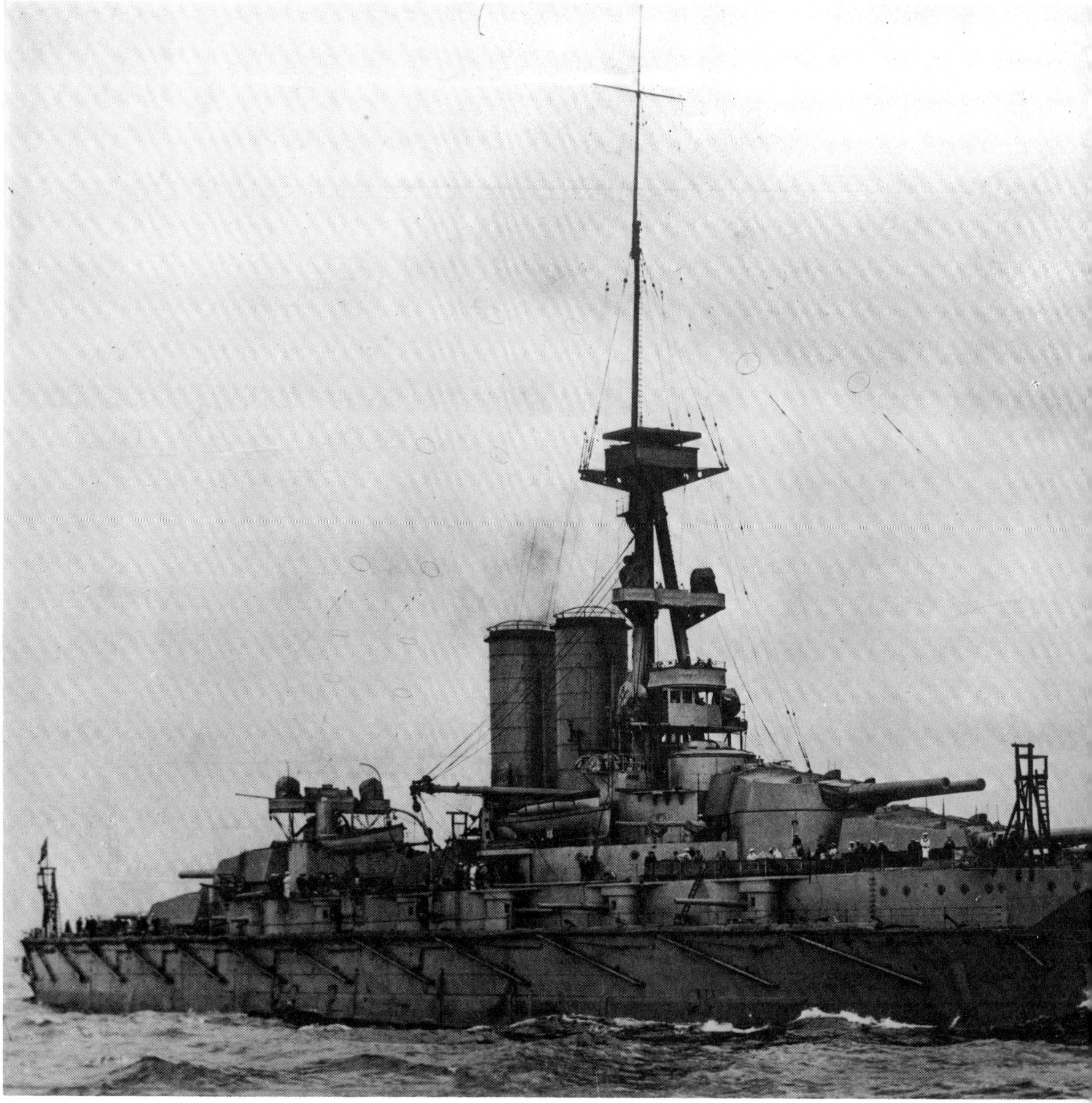

Left: *Erin* running speed trials in August 1914. She was originally built for the Turkish Navy and named *Reshad V*, which was later changed to *Reshadieh*. Launched at Vickers Shipyard in Barrow by the daughter of the Turkish Ambassador, she was fitting out and going through her working up period when war broke out. She was taken over by the Royal Navy and renamed *Erin* on entering service with the 4th Battle Squadron of the Grand Fleet. The vessel needed very little modification to fit in with the rest of the British Fleet, and was regarded as equal to the British *King George V*, although she was rather cramped internally.
Top: *Erin* in the summer of 1914, showing her simple bridge platforms and high freeboard. The anti-torpedo nets were removed in the early months of 1915, as were those of most British battleships.
Below: *Erin* at the end of the war (1918/1919), showing little alteration since her completion except for the usual additions, such as searchlight towers and extra bridge platforms.

ERIN

Builder(s): Vickers Shipbuilding
Laid down: 6 December 1911
Launched: 3 September 1913
Completed: July 1914

Displacement
Normal condition: 23,000 tons
Deep load: 25,470 tons

Dimensions
Length: 525ft (between perpendiculars); 559ft 6in (overall)
Beam: 91ft 7in
Draught: 28ft 6in (normal); 31ft (deep)

Armament (as completed)
10-13.5in 45-calibre
16-6in 50-calibre
6-6pdr
2-12pdr (8cwt)
4-21in torpedo tubes

Armour protection
Main belt: 12in
Upper belt: 8in
End belts: 6in-4in
Bulkheads: 8in-5in-4in
Barbettes: 10in-9in-5in-3in
Conning tower: 12in-4in
Forecastle: 1½in
Upper deck: 1½in
Main deck: 1½in
Middle deck: 1in-3in
Anti-torpedo protection: 1½in

Machinery
Parsons direct-drive turbines with four screws
15 Babcock and Wilcox boilers
26,500shp for a speed of 21 knots

Fuel and endurance
900 tons of coal (normal); 2,120 tons (maximum)
Endurance: 5,300 miles at 10 knots

Complement
1,070-1,130

Fate(s)
Scrapped from December 1922.

Note
Erin was originally laid down for the Turkish Navy in 1911 as *Reshad V*, but was later renamed *Reshadieh*. On the outbreak of war in 1914, she was taken over by the Royal Navy and renamed *Erin*.

AGINCOURT

Builder(s): Armstrongs, Elswick
Laid down: 14 September 1911
Launched: 22 January 1913
Completed: 20 August 1914

Displacement
Normal condition: 27,740 tons
Deep load: 31,620 tons

Dimensions
Length: 632ft (waterline); 671ft 6in (overall)
Beam: 89ft
Draught: 28ft 1in (normal); 30ft 6in (deep)

Armament (as completed)
14-12in 45-calibre
20-6in 50-calibre
10-3in
4-3pdr
3-12in torpedo tubes

Armour protection
Main belt: 9in
Upper belt: 6in
End belts: 6in-4in
Bulkheads: 6in-3in
Barbettes: 9in-3in
Turrets: 12in-8in
Conning tower: 12in
Forecastle: 1½in
Upper deck: 1½in
Main deck: 1in-1½in
Middle deck: 1in-1½in
Anti-torpedo protection: 1in-1½in

Machinery
Parsons direct-drive turbines with four screws
22 Babcock and Wilcox boilers
34,000shp for a speed of 22 knots

Fuel and endurance
1,500 tons of coal (normal); 3,200 tons (maximum)
Endurance: 4,000 miles at 10 knots (estimated)

Complement
1,115-1,267

Fate(s)
Scrapped from December 1924.

Note
Agincourt carried the largest number of 12in guns ever mounted in a British battleship. She was originally laid down for the Brazilian Navy, sold to Turkey, and finally taken over by the Royal Navy on the outbreak of war. First named *Rio de Janeiro* by the Brazilian Navy, she was renamed *Sultan Osman I* by the Turks, and in August 1914 named *Agincourt* by the Royal Navy.

Below: The magnificent, unique *Agincourt* on completion at Devonport in July 1914. She was originally ordered by the Brazilian Navy as the *Rio de Janeiro* during a period of intense rivalry in battleship construction between Argentina, Brazil and Chile. Financial problems caused her sale to Turkey, whereupon she was renamed *Sultan Osman 1*. Turkey paid £2,225,000 for the vessel, but almost crippled herself financially in the process. Nearing completion on the outbreak of war, she was taken over by the Royal Navy, removed from the yard of Armstrong Whitworth and sent to Devonport in an incomplete condition, as will be seen in the photograph; note that the guns of 'Thursday' ('X') turret are missing. (Each of the vessel's seven turrets were named after a day of the week.) She was renamed *Agincourt* on entering service with the Royal Navy, and returned to the Tyne where she completed her full armament complement in the first week of August 1914. She joined the Grand Fleet at sea on 25 August 1914 as a unit of the 4th Battle Squadron. The massive flying decks amidships were removed shortly after her appropriation by the Royal Navy, to prevent the possibility of them fouling the 12in turrets below if they were damaged. At the time, she was considered the most powerfully armed warship in the world.

Right, top: *Agincourt* towards the end of the war, 1918. Compare this view with that of her as completed; the first and most noticeable change is that the aft tripod has been removed. Other changes include a new large foretop, searchlight towers around the aft funnel, and topmast alterations.

Right, below: *Valparaiso* (later renamed *Almirante Latorre*) was ordered from Armstrong-Whitworth by the Chilean Government. She was a direct reply to the Brazilian Navy's *Rio de Janeiro* (later *Agincourt*). The Chilean naval staff favoured a smaller number of large-calibre guns, in contrast to the Brazilians' preference for seven turrets, which required a much longer hull. Also taken over by the Royal Navy on the outbreak of war, she was renamed *Canada*. In her case, however, it was always the intention to return her after the cessation of hostilities. *Canada* is seen here in the early war years (c.1915/16) with her anti-torpedo nets removed. She was one of the few ships whose basic appearance remained almost unchanged throughout her 45 years service.

CANADA

Builder(s): Armstrongs, Elswick
Laid down: December 1911
Launched: 27 November 1913
Completed: September 1915

Displacement
Normal condition: 28,622 tons
Deep load: 32,188 tons

Dimensions
Length: 654ft 10in (waterline); 661ft (overall)
Beam: 92ft
Draught: 29ft 6in (normal); 31ft 11in (deep)

Armament (as completed)
10-14in 45-calibre Mark 1
16-6in 50-calibre
4-3pdr
2-12pdr field-gun
4 machine-guns
4-21in torpedo tubes

Armour protection
Main belt: 9in
Upper belt: 4in
End belts: 6in-4in
Bulkheads: 4in
Barbettes: 10in-6in-4in
Turrets: 10in
Conning tower: 11in
Forecastle: 1in
Upper deck: 1½in
Main deck: 1½in
Middle deck: 1in-4in
Shelter: 1in
Anti-torpedo protection: 1¼-2in

Machinery
Mixture of Brown and Curtis and Parsons direct-drive turbines with four screws
21 Yarrow boilers
37,000shp for a speed of 22.75 knots

Fuel and endurance
1,150 tons of coal (normal); 3,330 tons (maximum)
Endurance: 4,400 miles at 10 knots (coal only)

Complement
1,151

Fate(s)
After serving with the Chilean Navy for many years, *Canada* was finally sold and taken to Japan for scrapping. She arrived at Tokyo Bay in August 1959, making her the longest surviving battleship to have served at Jutland in 1916.

Note
She was originally built for the Chilean Navy as *Almirante Latorre*, but was taken over by the Royal Navy at the outbreak of the First World War and renamed *Canada*. She was handed back to Chile in April 1920, whereupon she readopted her original name.

Left: *Canada* shortly before the end of the war in 1918. Her sister-ship *Almirante Cochrane*, ordered at the same time as *Canada*, was left on the stocks at the outbreak of war and was not taken over by the Royal Navy until 1917. She was then converted into an aircraft carrier and renamed *Eagle*.
Centre left: *Canada* at sea, 1915–16. This photograph affords a good view of the ship's flat-sided funnels, which were of unequal thickness and some of the tallest ever fitted in a battleship.
Below: *Canada*, showing her flying-off platforms, June 1919. She is seen here in Reserve, after the disbandment of the Grand Fleet in April 1919.

Top: A splendid view of *Canada* taken from the air by the newly-formed Aerial Photographic Department of the Royal Air Force, 1917–18. Note the spaciousness of her layout, which allowed *Canada* to be known as a comfortable ship.
Above and right: *Canada* in 1931, now returned to the Chilean Navy and given her original name *Almirante Latorre*. She is seen here coming into Devonport for a major refit, when she was given new machinery, underwater protection in the form of bulges, plus regular improvements such as a new bridge structure and internal changes to the living-quarters.

Left: Queen Elizabeth taking part in the Dardanelles Campaign on 18 March 1915, shortly after her completion. Her 15in guns are firing indirectly at a heavily protected gun fort, although as the spotting and range of the target were almost impossible to calculate, the vessel was, in fact, wasting her time. However, she did succeed in hitting one of the forts, knocking out some of the heavy guns installed there.

QUEEN ELIZABETH CLASS

Name of ship:	Queen Elizabeth	Warspite	Barham	Valiant	Malaya
Builder(s):	Portsmouth Royal Docks	Devonport Royal Docks	John Brown Shipyard	Fairfield Shipbuilders	Armstrongs, Elswick
Laid down:	21 October 1912	31 October 1912	24 February 1913	31 January 1913	20 October 1913
Launched:	16 October 1913	26 November 1913	31 December 1914	4 November 1914	18 March 1915
Completed:	January 1915	March 1915	October 1915	February 1916	February 1916

Displacement
Normal condition: 27,500 tons (designed)
Deep load: over 33,000 tons (actual); 31,350 tons (designed)

Dimensions
Length: 600ft (between perpendiculars); 639ft-643ft (overall)
Beam: 90ft 6in
Draught: 28ft 9in (normal); 32ft 1in (deep, designed), 32-33ft (deep, actual)

Armament (as completed)
8-15in 42-calibre
16-6in 50-calibre (reduced after *Queen Elizabeth*)
4-3pdr
5 machine-guns
4-12in torpedo tubes

Armour protection
Main belt: 13in
Upper belt: 6in
End belts: 4in
Bulkheads: 6in-4in
Barbettes: 10in-7in-6in
Turrets: 13in-11in
Conning tower: 11in
Main deck: 1¼in
Middle deck: 1in
Lower deck: 1in-3in
Anti-torpedo protection: 2in

Machinery
Brown and Curtis turbines (*Barham* and *Valiant*); Parsons turbines (*Queen Elizabeth*, *Warspite* and *Malaya*)
24 Babcock and Wilcox boilers (*Malaya*, *Queen Elizabeth* and *Warspite*); Yarrow boilers (*Barham* and *Valiant*)

Fuel and endurance
650 tons of oil (normal); 3,400 tons (maximum)
Endurance: 6,450 miles at 10 knots

Complement
923-1,016

Fate(s)
Queen Elizabeth, scrapped from 1948.
Warspite, scrapped from 1949/50.
Barham, sunk by a U-boat in the Mediterranean on 25 November 1941; her magazines exploded after she had received three hits.
Valiant, scrapped from 1949.
Malaya, scrapped from 1948.

Note
The ships of this class were the first to mount 15in guns and, on completion, were considered to be the best battleships in the world. All served in the Second World War after reconstruction.

Right: Another view of *Queen Elizabeth* at the Dardanelles. The splash near the stern of the ship indicates that she was under fire from the enemy forts. Although no serious damage was caused to the vessel, it was later decided that *Queen Elizabeth* was far too valuable to risk in such an action and she was withdrawn from the scene.

Centre right: *Barham*, 1920/21, giving a clear view of the 15in guns in 'X' turret, and the ship's Sopwith Camel being manoeuvred into position on the runway. At this time she was the flagship of the 2nd Battle Squadron of the Atlantic Fleet.

Below left: *Queen Elizabeth* after the war, 1918/19. Note the large control top with short topmasts fitted. The bridges and platforms have been altered since 1915 to allow for the usual additions received throughout the war. The class could be told apart by a close study of the searchlight arrangement at the base of the mainmast which was located at different heights. The topmasts and rig were also different. The 6in secondary guns fitted in *Barham* and *Queen Elizabeth* on completion were removed from the upper deck level shortly afterwards, leaving only those on the middle deck in casemates.

Below right: *Malaya* paying a special visit to the country that paid for her construction in 1915. She is fully dressed for this courtesy visit to the Malayan states, where she arrived in December 1920 and stayed until March 1921.

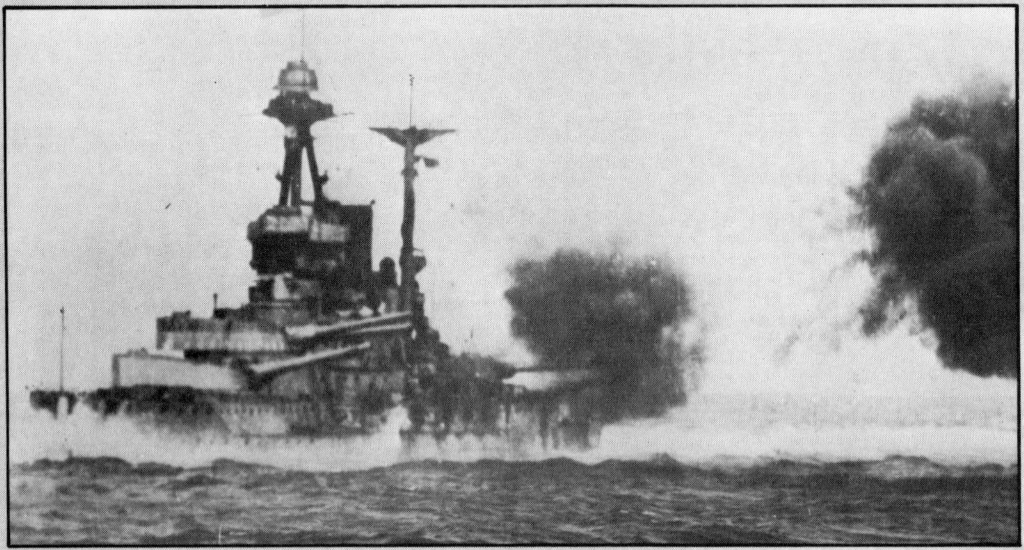

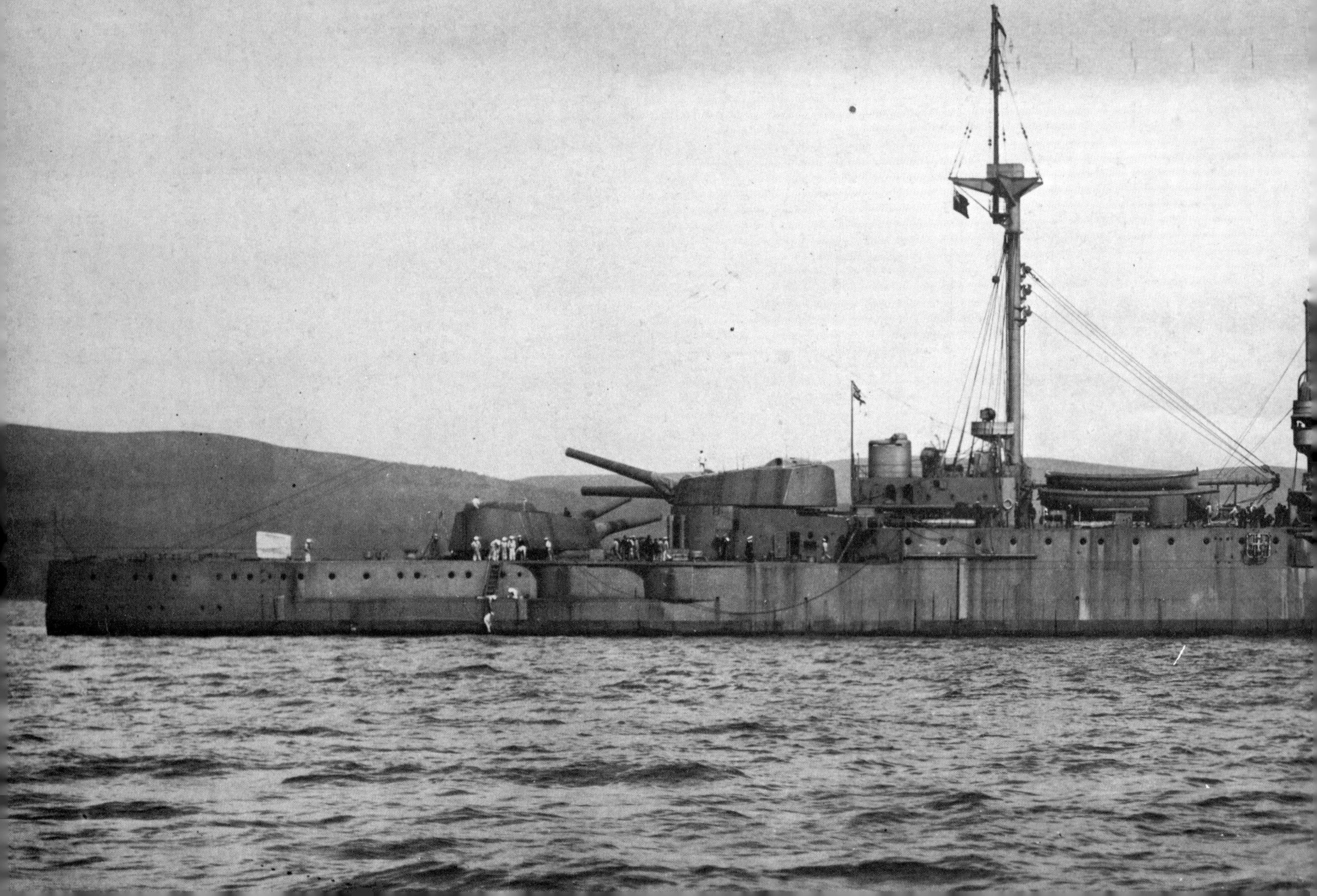

Left: *Barham* opens fire with her 15in guns, c.1918 perhaps late 1917. *Barham* was a unit of the famous 5th Battle Squadron which had distinguished itself at Jutland in 1916 by practically saving the British battlecruiser force from destruction.
Below: *Barham* having left John Brown's Shipyard after completion in 1915. The vessels of the *Queen Elizabeth* class were always considered good-looking ships with excellent fighting qualities and quite equal to any contemporary adversary then in existence.
Right: A superb view of *Barham*, 1922/23. Note that she is carrying a rather tall topmast again. *Malaya*, *Valiant* and *Queen Elizabeth* also sported this fitting, but *Warspite* did not.

Above: *Queen Elizabeth* on 21 November 1918, leading the surrendered German High Seas Fleet into Scapa Flow after the cessation of hostilities. It was a magnificent spectacle, with the German High Seas Fleet flanked on both sides by the Grand Fleet, the Northern and Southern Lines, all battleships and battlecruisers. Cruisers and destroyers were also present, darting in and out of the three main columns.
Left: *Barham* in the spring of 1918, showing various wartime modifications. Note the small mast on the mainmast and the searchlight towers around the second funnel, although she has retained the lamp on the mainmast. The old 6in gun ports aft have been plated up.
Below left: *Queen Elizabeth* entering Portsmouth Harbour late in 1918. This was her first visit to the port since war had ended, and she was given a splendid reception on arrival.
Top right: *Queen Elizabeth* showing her flying-off platforms, 1919/20. The rangefinder clocks forward are clearly visible below the director tower, with those aft just visible near 'X' turret.
Below right: *Queen Elizabeth* emerges after a major refit in 1928, bound for the Mediterranean and her role as fleet flagship. The reconstruction took place at Portsmouth from May 1926 until August 1927. The forward funnel has been trunked into the aft uptake, giving the ship a rather heavy and stumpy appearance. Anti-torpedo bulges were added which increased the beam to approximately 104ft. The control top was enlarged, the after control top removed, extra 4in AA guns added port and starboard, an after pair of torpedo tubes removed and searchlight arrangements altered.

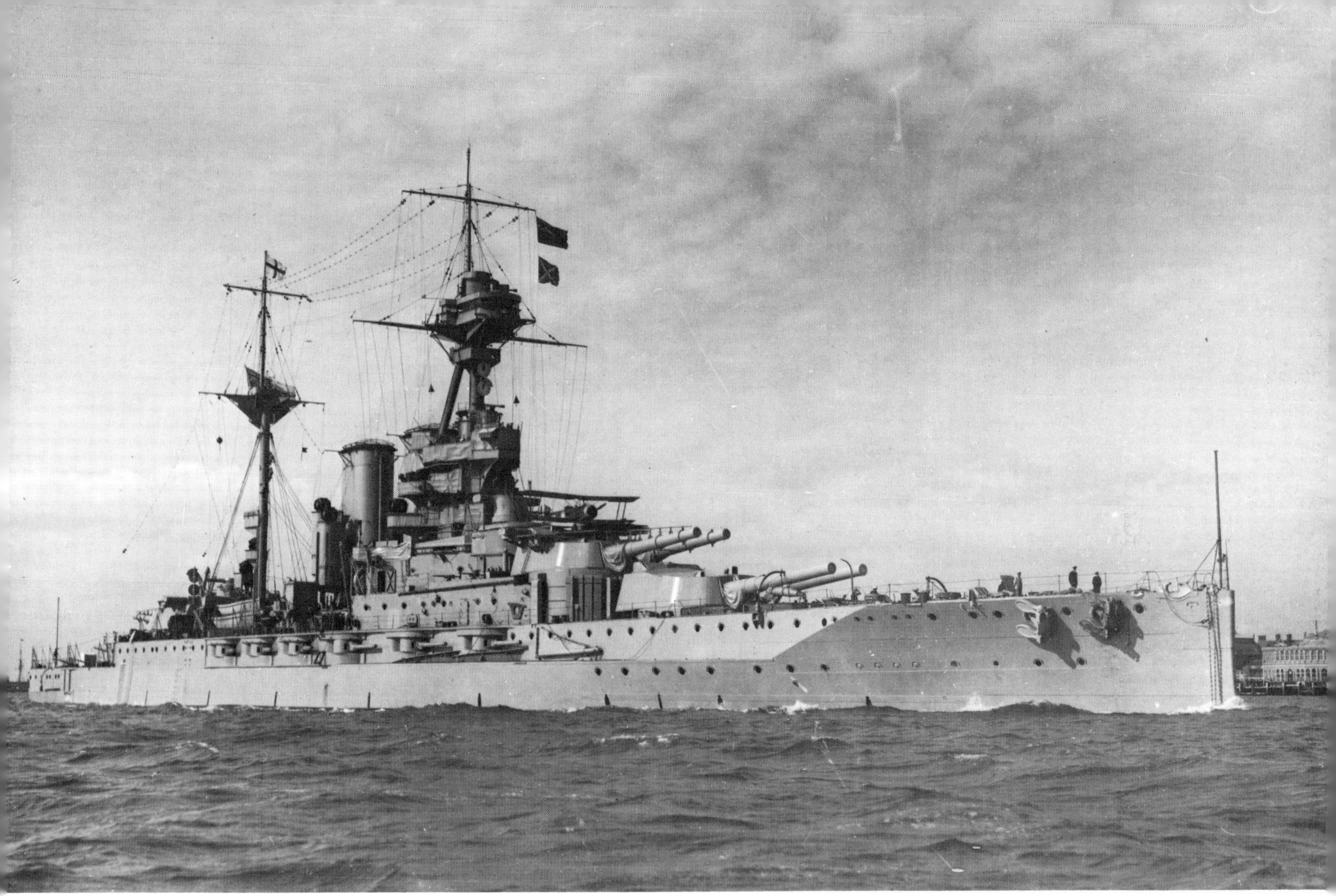

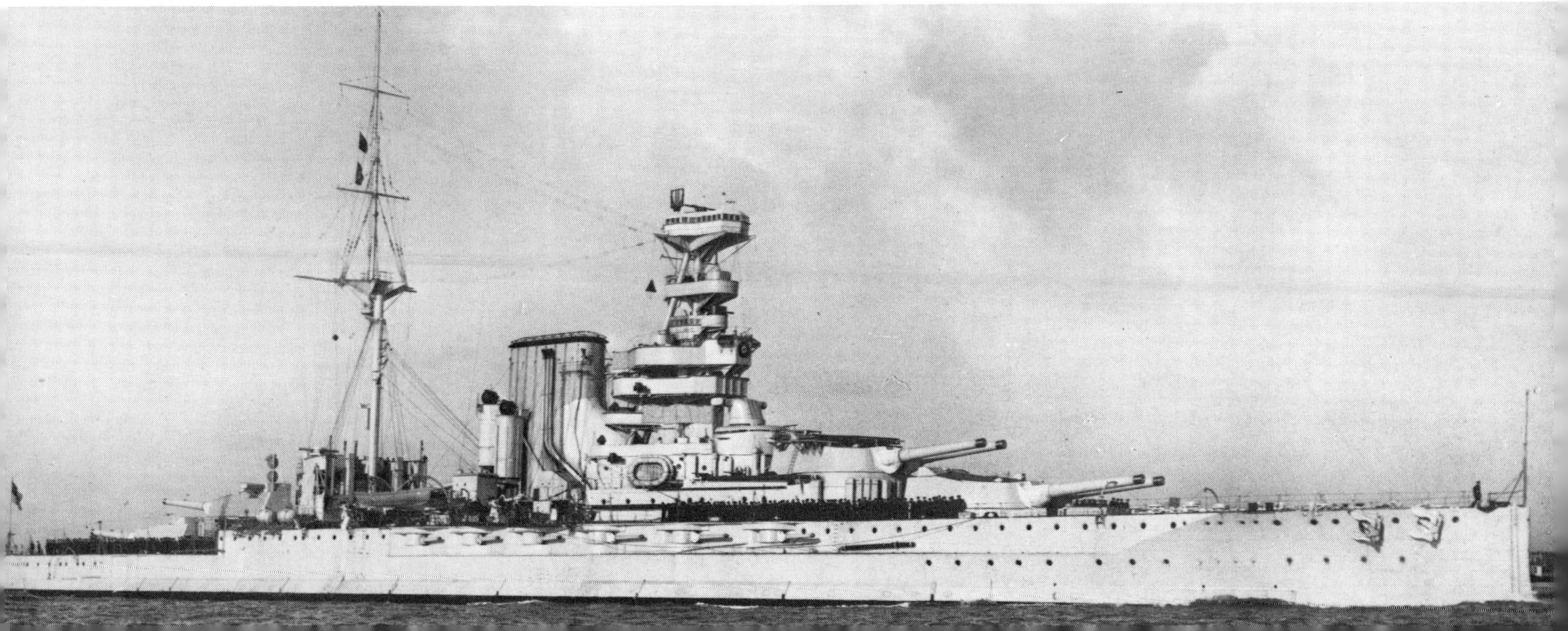

70

Far left, top: *Queen Elizabeth* entering Valetta Harbour on 21 July 1936. Additions to the vessel since reconstruction include rangefinders, extra parts to the bridges and improved wireless aerials. *Queen Elizabeth* had previously been stationed at Alexandria from October 1935 until the above date, during the Italo-Ethiopian crisis.
Far left, below: A splendid view of *Warspite* at Portsea in October 1933, showing her mid-thirties look. *Warspite's* modifications were along the same lines as those fitted in *Queen Elizabeth*. The refit lasted from October 1924 until April 1926, making her the first vessel of the class to be given this treatment. She was flagship of the 2nd Battle Squadron with the Home Fleet when the photograph was taken.
Below centre: In the mid-thirties it was decided to give facelifts to some of the best dreadnoughts, with the *Queen Elizabeth* class having priority because of their good condition. They were completely rebuilt from 'A' 15in gun turret through to 'Y' turret. *Warspite*, shown here amidships, is undergoing this reconstruction, which started in March 1934 and lasted until June 1937.
Left: A bow-on view of the completely reconstructed *Warspite*, 1937/38. This view shows to good effect the huge box-type superstructure, which housed everything that the older tripod mast had carried: navigating platform, bridges and conning tower with rangefinder located on the top. The new foremast was the old mainmast reduced in height and repositioned. Note the multiple pom-poms on 'B' 15in turret.
Below: *Warspite* entering the approaches to Valetta Harbour on 14 January 1938, to relieve *Barham* as Fleet Flagship of the Mediterranean.

Top: *Repulse* sailing down the Clyde on completion in September 1916. A beautiful class, *Repulse* and *Renown* were matched for looks only by *Tiger*. Their short, equal-height funnels and long, flared hulls gave them a unique appearance. The fore funnel was raised after the first steam trials and the ships entered service in this condition. Fortunately, this did not spoil their balanced appearance as it had with some other vessels. *Repulse* and *Renown* were almost identical on completion except for the following: *Repulse* had an open navigating platform while in *Renown* it was enclosed. *Repulse* had taller steampipes to the second funnel than those in *Renown*. The searchlight platforms around the funnels were identical in both ships as completed, but in 1917 *Renown* was fitted with a single platform, low down around the second funnel. *Repulse* was not similarly altered, making identification easy after this date.

Right: *Repulse* on completion leaving John Brown's shipyard for her preliminary steam trials in September 1916. Note the rows of scuttles along the ship's side, which reveal her lack of armoured freeboard. This feature made the class very unpopular, especially when the memory of Jutland was still fresh; three battlecruisers had been lost there, possibly because of their thin armour-plating, so the arrival of *Repulse* and *Renown* was not particularly reassuring.

73

RENOWN CLASS

Name of ship:	*Renown*	*Repulse*
Builder(s):	Fairfield Shipyard	John Brown Shipyard
Laid down:	25 January 1915	25 January 1915
Launched:	4 March 1916	8 January 1916
Completed:	20 September 1916	August 1916

Displacement
Normal condition: 26,548 tons
Deep load: 31,592 tons (*Renown*); 32,220 tons (*Repulse*)

Dimensions
Length: 750ft (between perpendiculars); 794ft (overall)
Beam: 90ft
Draught: 25ft 6in (normal); 29ft 7in (deep), 30ft 1in (*Repulse*)

Armament (as completed)
6-15in 42-calibre
17-4in 40-calibre
2-3in 50-calibre AA
1-12pdr (8cwt)
5 machine-guns
10 Lewis guns
2-21in torpedo tubes

Armour protection
Main belt: 6in
End belts: 4in (forward), 3in (aft)
Bulkheads: 4in-3in
Barbettes: 7in-5in-4in
Turrets: 11in-9in
Conning tower: 10in
Forecastle: ¾in-1⅛in
Upper deck: ½in-$\frac{7}{16}$in
Main deck: ¾in-1in-3in
Lower deck: ¾in-2½in
Anti-torpedo protection: Internal bulges fitted

Machinery
Brown and Curtis direct-drive turbines with four screws
42 Babcock and Wilcox boilers
112,000shp for speed of 31.5 knots

Fuel and endurance
1,000 tons of oil (minimum); 4,243 tons (maximum)
Endurance: 4,200 miles at 10 knots

Complement
953-1,016

Fate(s)
Repulse, sunk by Japanese bombers after being hit by at least five torpedoes, 10 December 1941.
Renown, scrapped from Faslane, then to Troon, 1948–49.

Note
These vessels did not live up to expectations on completion, although a series of refits did improve them considerably.

Above: A close-up of the fore funnel and superstructure of *Repulse* in December 1918. She is wearing a unique, one-off type of camouflage composed of dark grey splashes along the vessel, bearing no resemblance to the Dazzle that was popular then. Part of the camouflage can be seen here on the funnels. Note that the early searchlight platforms fitted to the funnels on completion have now been removed; the lamps have been repositioned on the searchlight towers around the second funnel.

Top right: A port bow view of *Renown*, late 1918. *Repulse* and *Renown* are very hard to tell apart at certain angles, but a close examination of their superstructures does provide the answer. One feature to look for is the short topmast, which was fitted on *Renown* during this period but not *Repulse*.

Right: An excellent starboard view of *Repulse* entering Portsmouth Harbour in late 1918 for her large refit, when the main armoured belt was increased from 6in to 9in. *Repulse* was the first large warship to enter Portsmouth Harbour after the war had ended. She is wearing the same unusual camouflage scheme already mentioned, although it is not very obvious.

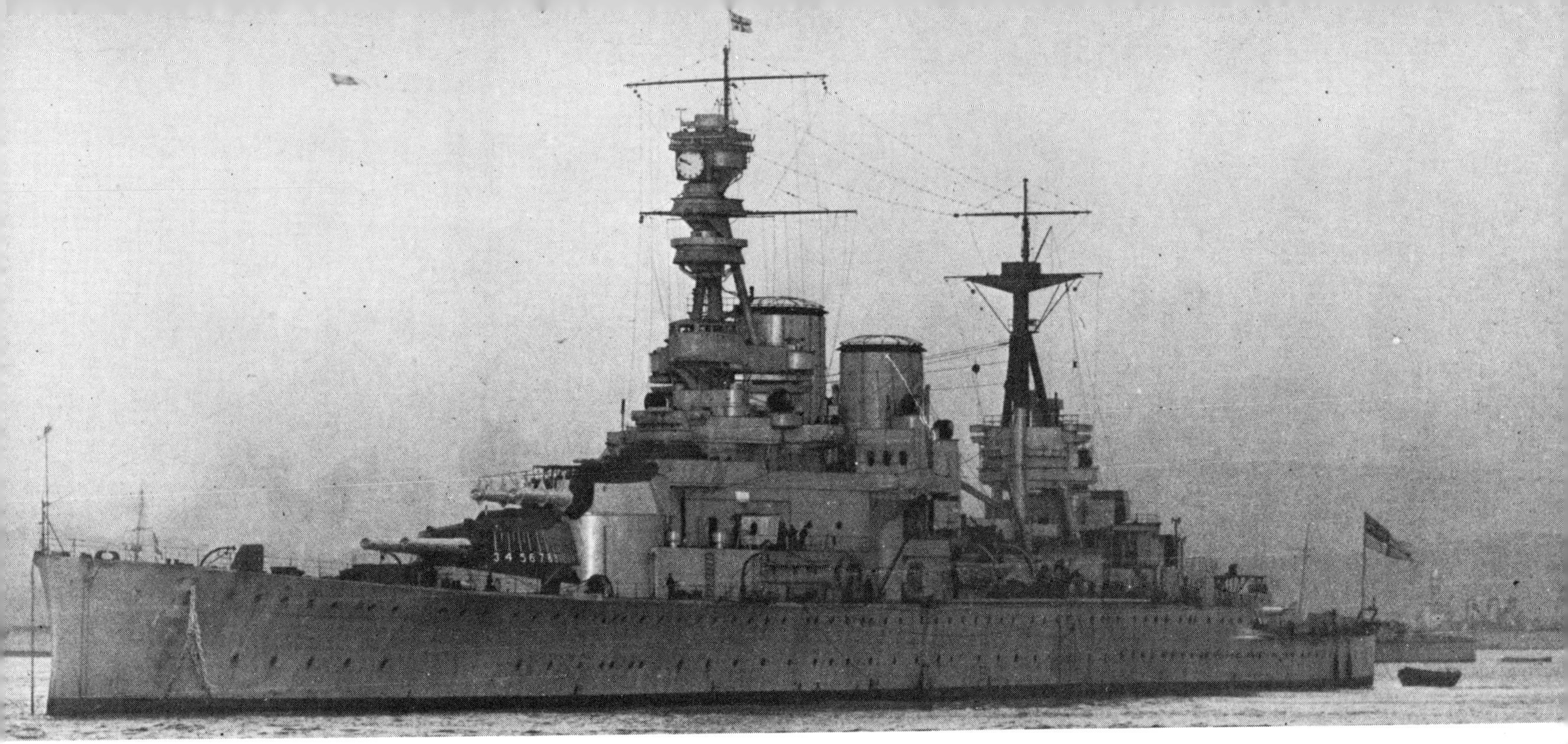

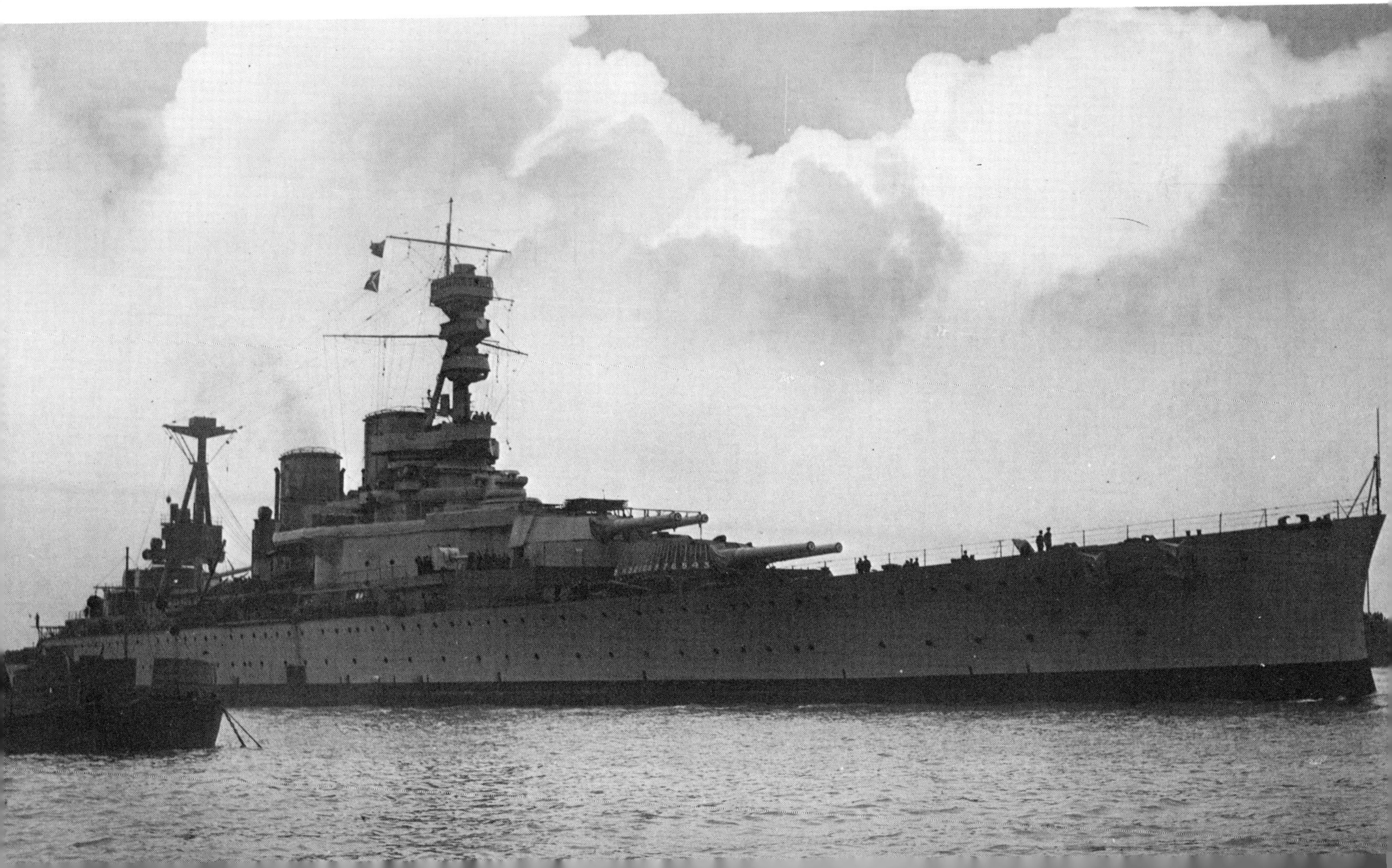

Above: *Renown* with HRH the Prince of Wales on board during a Royal cruise, arriving at Auckland, New Zealand on 24 April 1920. *Renown* fulfilled the role of Royal Yacht on many occasions and, in this guise, she visited faraway places such as Barbados, Honolulu, the Fiji Islands, Panama and New Zealand. This particular tour finished in Australia, with *Renown* finally returning to Great Britain in October 1920. Note the accommodation structures between the funnels which were built especially for the tours.

Below: *Renown* in June 1922. Compare this view with that of the vessel at war's end. The aircraft platforms have been removed and the bridge has a different face; she is without rangefinder clocks or scales on the turrets and a topgallant mast has been fitted. *Renown* still has the long rows of scuttles, unlike *Repulse* in this period.

Top right: The bows of *Repulse*, after her major refit in 1936. Note the new superstructure with wing supports and new crane amidships near the mainmast. She is seen here in June leaving Portsmouth for the Mediterranean where she joined the Battlecruiser Squadron.

Below right: *Renown* after her reconstruction, which lasted from September 1936 until the summer of 1939. She emerged from the builder's yard at Portsmouth virtually a new ship, and although she had lost her classic appearance, she could still boast of being a well designed and evenly balanced vessel. This photograph was taken in July 1939.

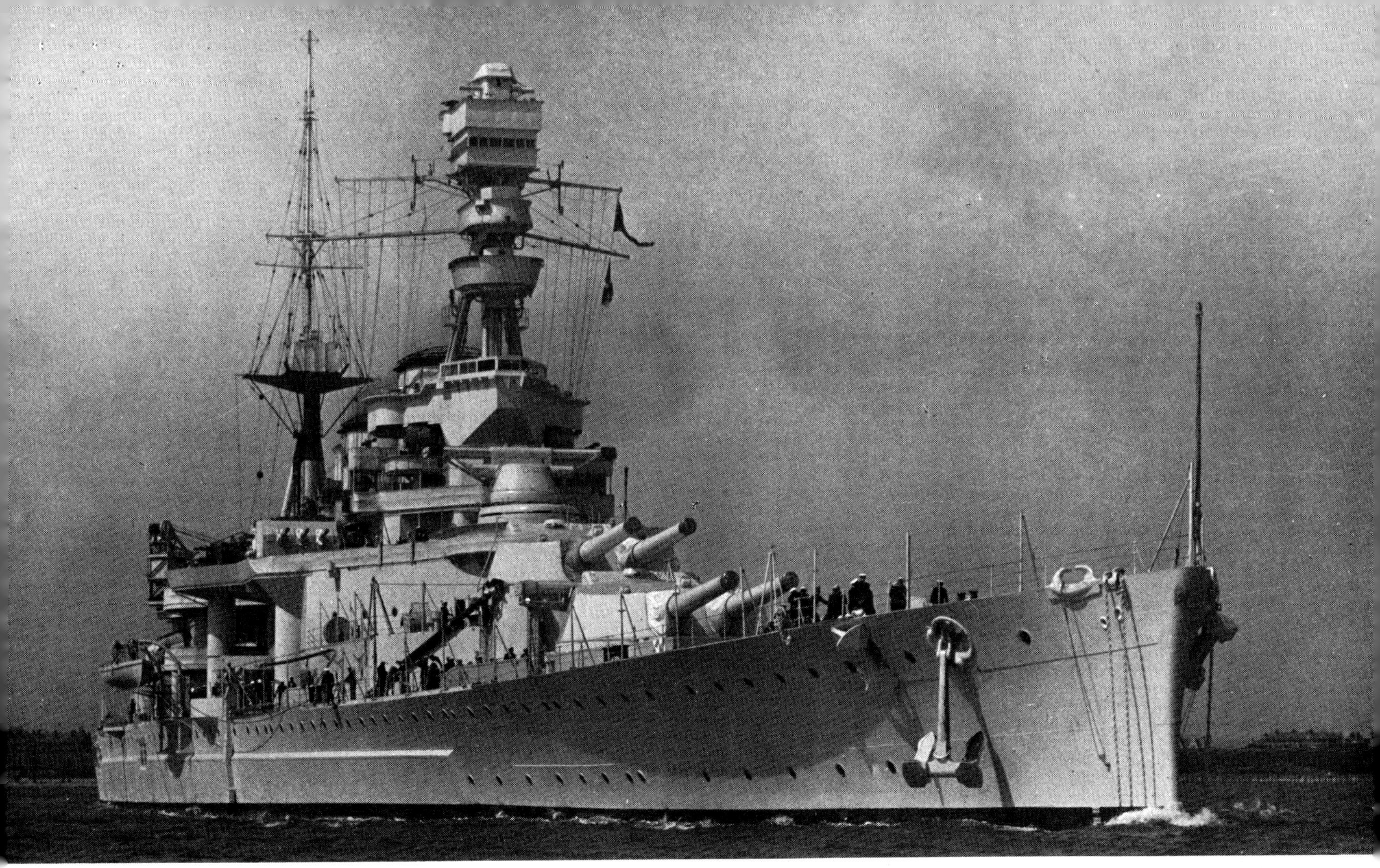

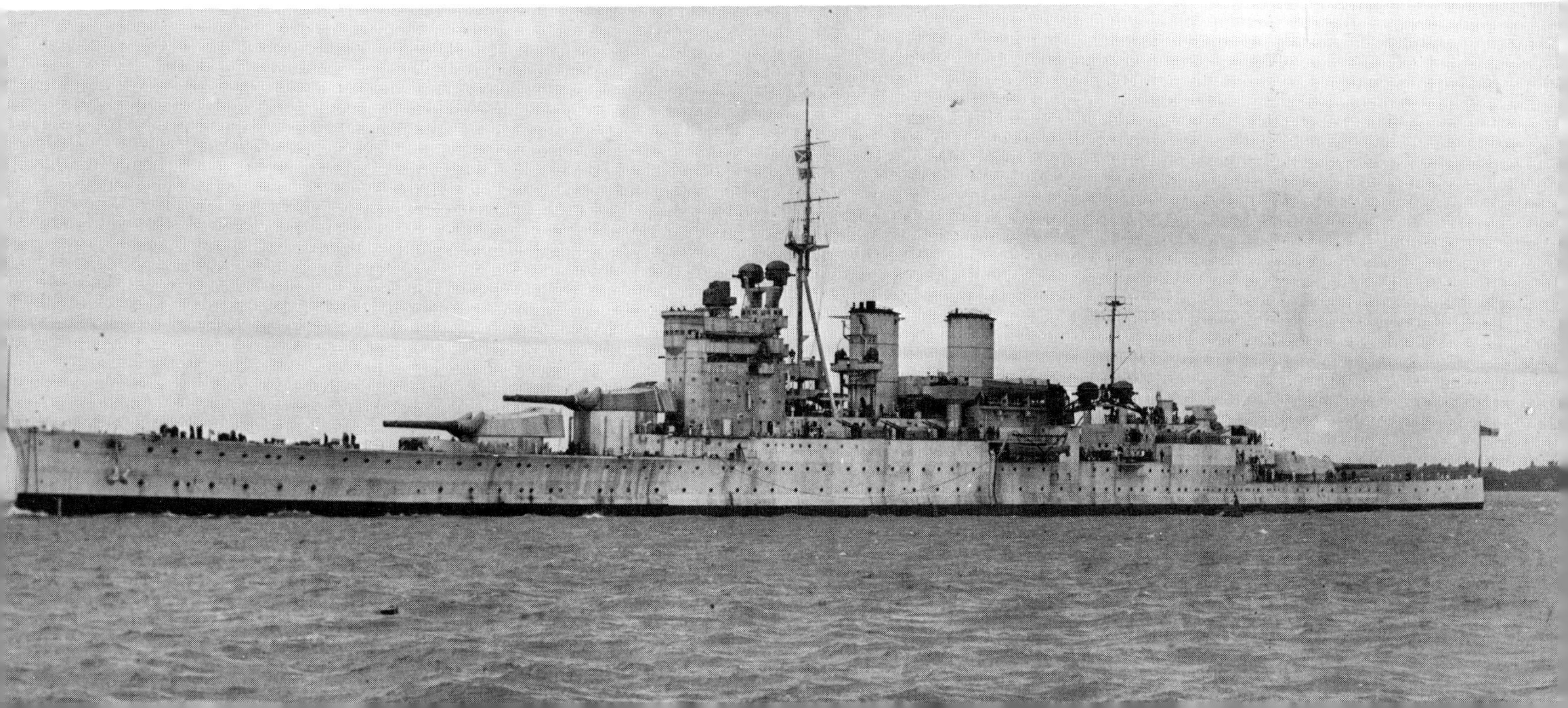

78

Far left, top: *Royal Sovereign* under construction at the Royal Dockyard at Portsmouth in 1913—14, with 'A' and 'B' turrets taking shape. Originally designed as 21-knot coal and oil burning ships with a designed 31,000 shaft horsepower, the *Royal Sovereign* class were modified while under construction to burn oil fuel only. The shaft horsepower was increased to 40,000 which, in turn, increased the designed speed to 23 knots. There was a reduction in the number of boilers compared with the *Queen Elizabeth* vessels (18 in *Royal Sovereign*, 24 in *Queen Elizabeth*), permitting the elimination of one of the uptakes and resulting in the appearance of the first British dreadnought to be built with one funnel.
Left: *Royal Sovereign*, seen from the deck of one of her sisters towards the end of the war in 1918. The black spot at the top of her foretop is a searchlight, a feature that the rest of the class did not share.
Below, left and right: *Ramillies* wearing her weird Dazzle camouflage as painted up in the winter of 1917. It was composed of seven different colours, including yellow and pink! Note that the scheme is not uniform on each side of the ship.

Above and left: *Revenge* in the summer of 1918, displaying her Dazzle camouflage, which is very different from that of her sister *Ramillies*. Apart from the difference in design, it is composed of blues, blacks and greys.
Right: *Royal Oak* passing *Victory* on entering Portsmouth after the war in 1918. *Royal Oak* and *Revenge* were the only two units of the class to serve at Jutland, the remaining three being still under construction.

ROYAL SOVEREIGN CLASS

Name of ship:	Royal Sovereign	Ramillies	Resolution	Revenge	Royal Oak
Builder(s):	Portsmouth Royal Docks	Beardmore Shipyard	Palmers Shipyard	Vickers Shipyard	Devonport Royal Docks
Laid down:	15 January 1914	12 November 1913	29 December 1913	22 December 1913	15 January 1914
Launched:	29 April 1915	12 September 1916	14 January 1915	29 May 1915	17 November 1914
Completed:	May 1916	September 1917	December 1916	May 1916	May 1916

Displacement
Normal condition: 29,970 tons
Deep load: 31,160 tons

Dimensions
Length: 580ft (between perpendiculars); 620ft (overall)
Beam: 88ft 6in
Draught: 30ft (normal); 33ft (deep)

Armament (as completed)
8-15in 42-calibre
14-6in 50-calibre
4-3pdr
5 machine-guns
4-12in torpedo tubes

Armour protection
Main belt: 13in
Upper belt: 6in
End belts: 6in-4in
Bulkheads: 6in-4in
Barbettes: 10in-9in-7in
Turrets: 13in-11in
Conning tower: 11in
Forecastle: 1in
Upper deck: 2in
Main deck: 2in
Middle deck: 2in-3in-4in
Anti-torpedo protection: 1in-1½in

Machinery
Originally intended to be coal-fuelled, they were changed to oil during the design stage.
Parsons direct-drive turbines with four screws
18 Babcock and Wilcox boilers (*Ramillies, Revenge* and *Royal Sovereign*); Yarrow boilers (*Resolution* and *Royal Oak*)
40,000shp for speed of 23 knots

Fuel and endurance
900 tons of oil (normal); 3,400 tons (maximum)
Endurance: 6,800 miles at 10 knots

Complement
920

Fate(s)
Royal Sovereign, scrapped from 1949.
Revenge, scrapped from 1949.
Resolution, scrapped from 1948.
Ramillies, scrapped from 1949.
Royal Oak, sunk by *U47* while at anchor in Scapa Flow, 14 October 1939.

Note
All but *Royal Oak* served throughout the Second World War. Unlike the *Queen Elizabeth* class, they never underwent major reconstruction.

Left: The forecastle of *Revenge*, c.1919–20, showing her anchor arrangements and turret tops. Note the aircraft platform on 'B' turret. *Revenge* was the first flagship of the Atlantic Fleet when this photograph was taken.

Right and overleaf: *Revenge* entering the Grand Harbour at Malta in January 1935. Compare her bridge with that of *Ramillies*; the class could be told apart by their bridges and anti-torpedo bulges. The bulges of *Royal Sovereign*, *Revenge* and *Resolution* were identical, shallow fittings just visible above the waterline. *Ramillies* and *Royal Oak* had huge, high fitting bulges that almost reached the 6in secondary battery level.

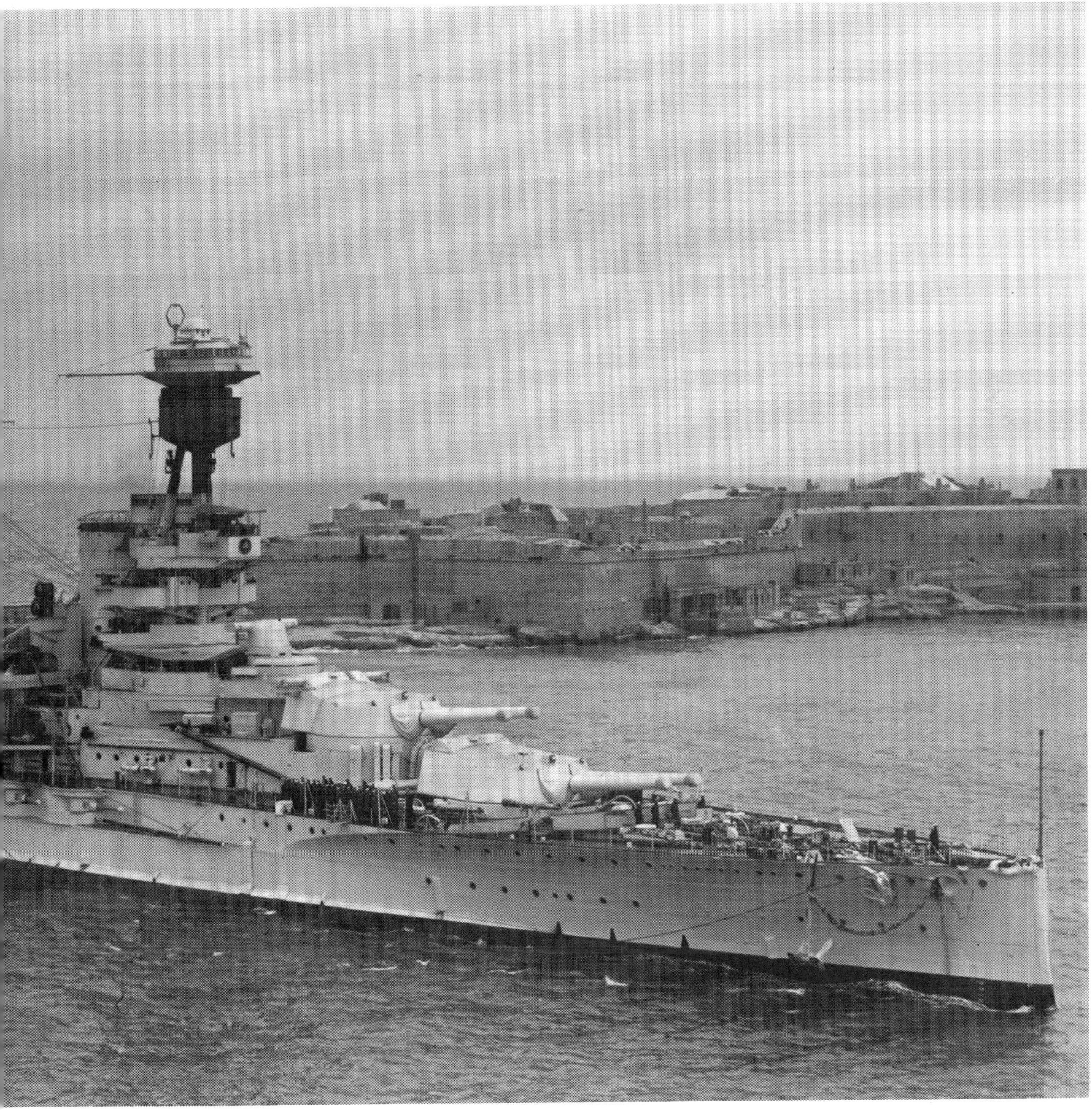

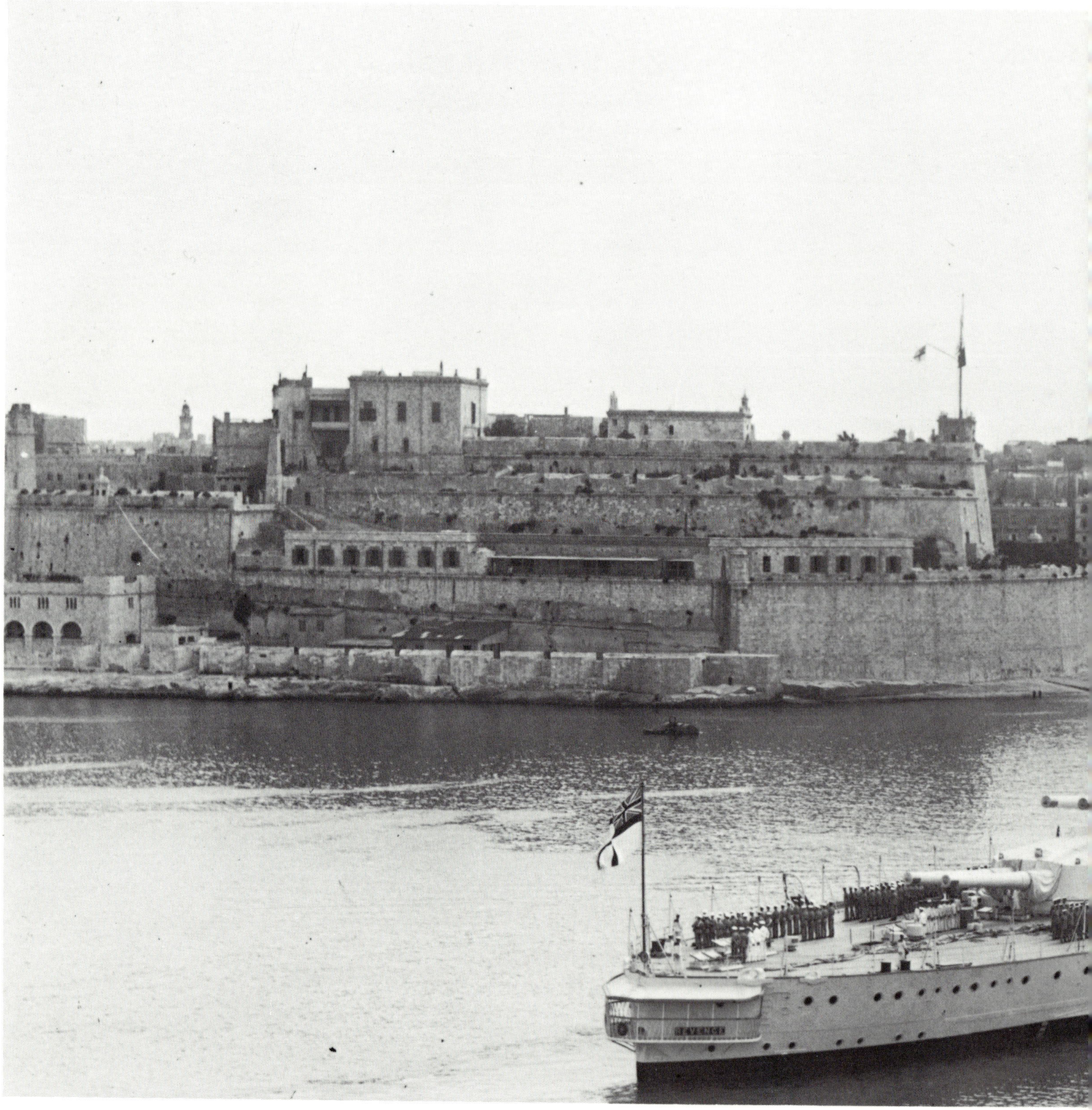
REVENGE

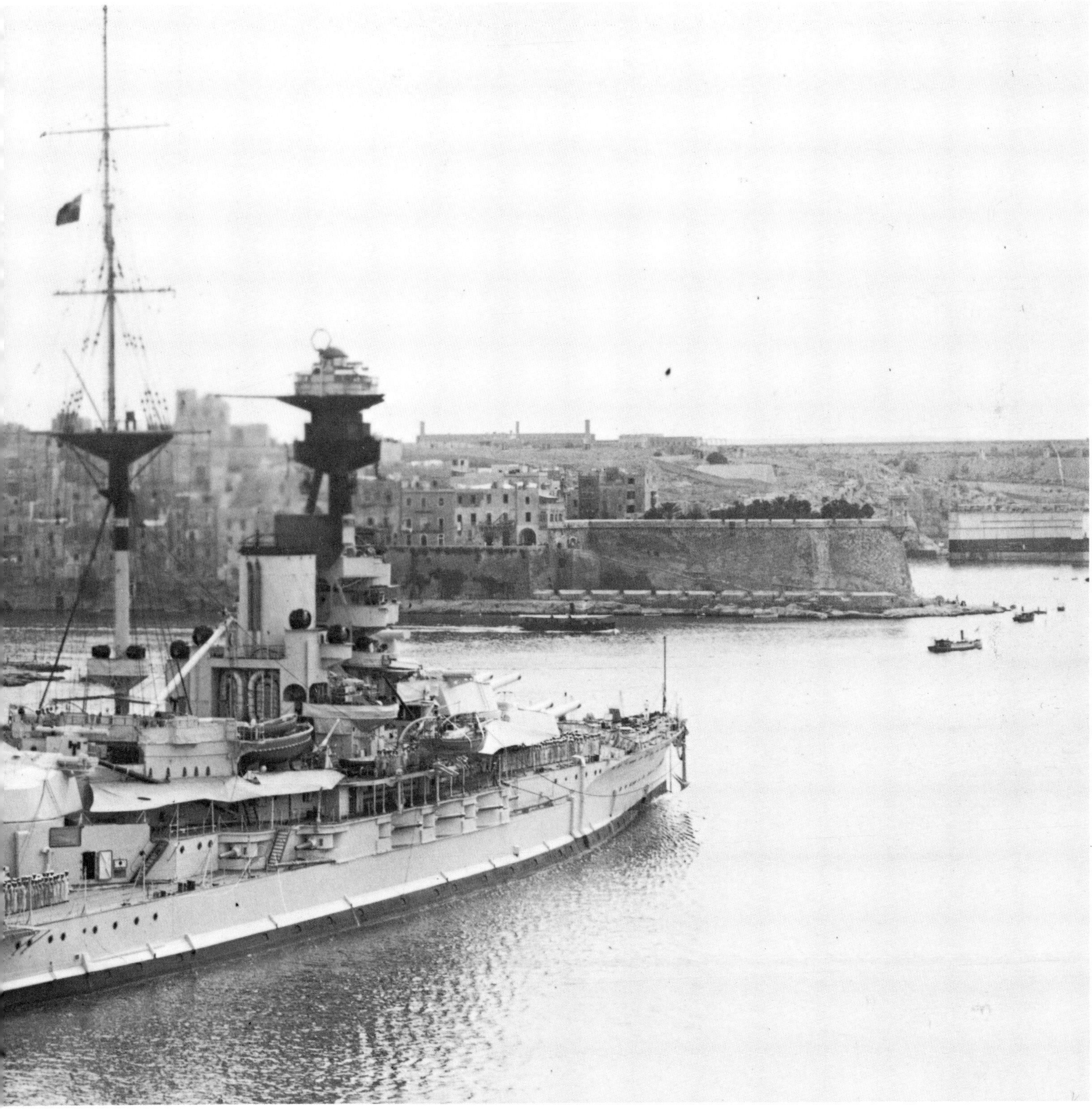

Above: *Ramillies* entering Valetta Harbour in February 1935. Note the many changes since her completion, which include new bridgework, searchlight towers, new enlarged foretop and, most prominent of all, the large anti-torpedo bulges fitted along the hull of the vessel.
Right: *Resolution* at Torbay in the early 1920s. Although the vessels of the *Royal Sovereign* class were never rated as highly as the previous *Queen Elizabeth* class (mainly due to the *Queen Elizabeths* higher speed) they were exceptionally well designed vessels and capable of great fighting efficiency.

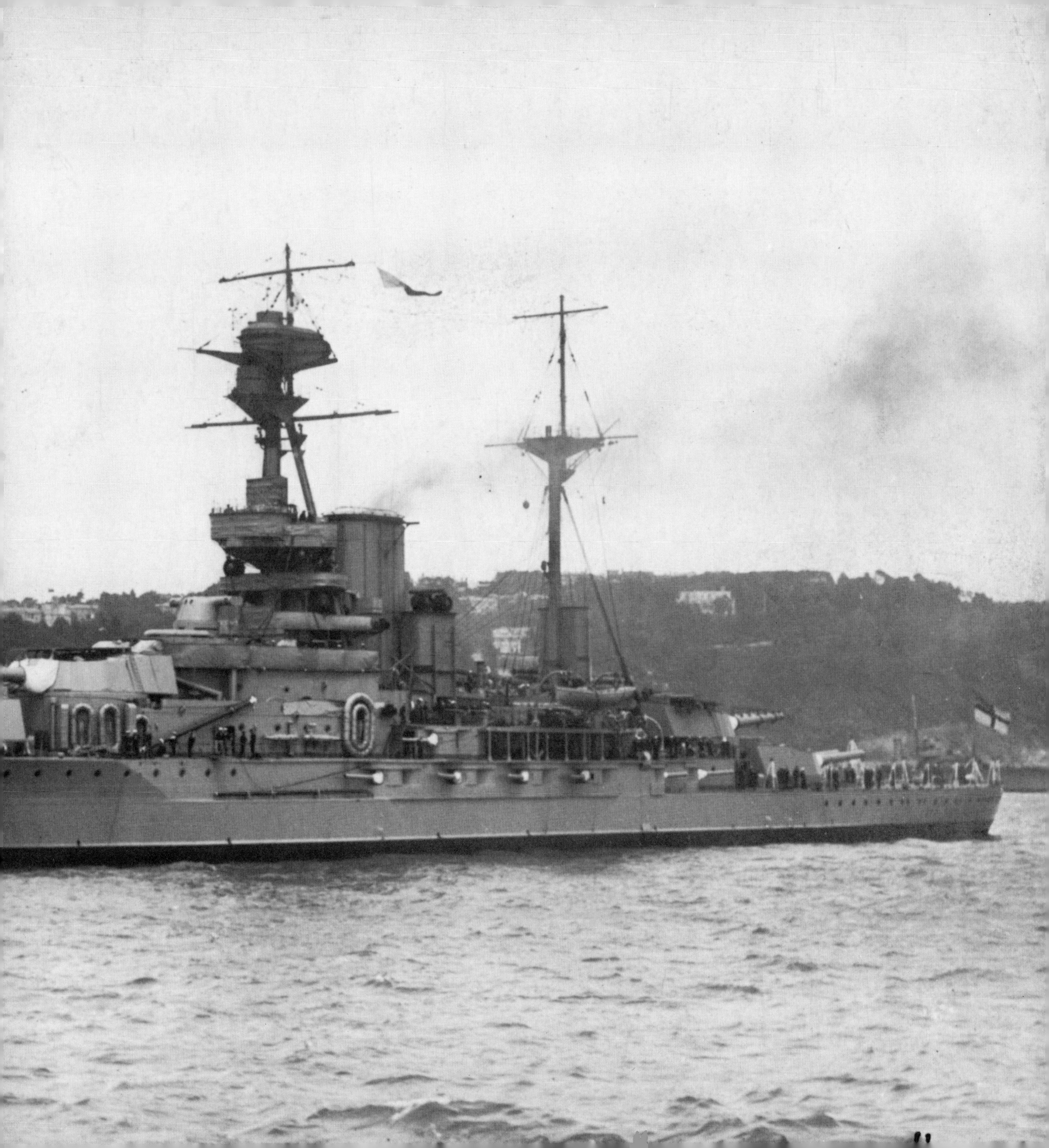

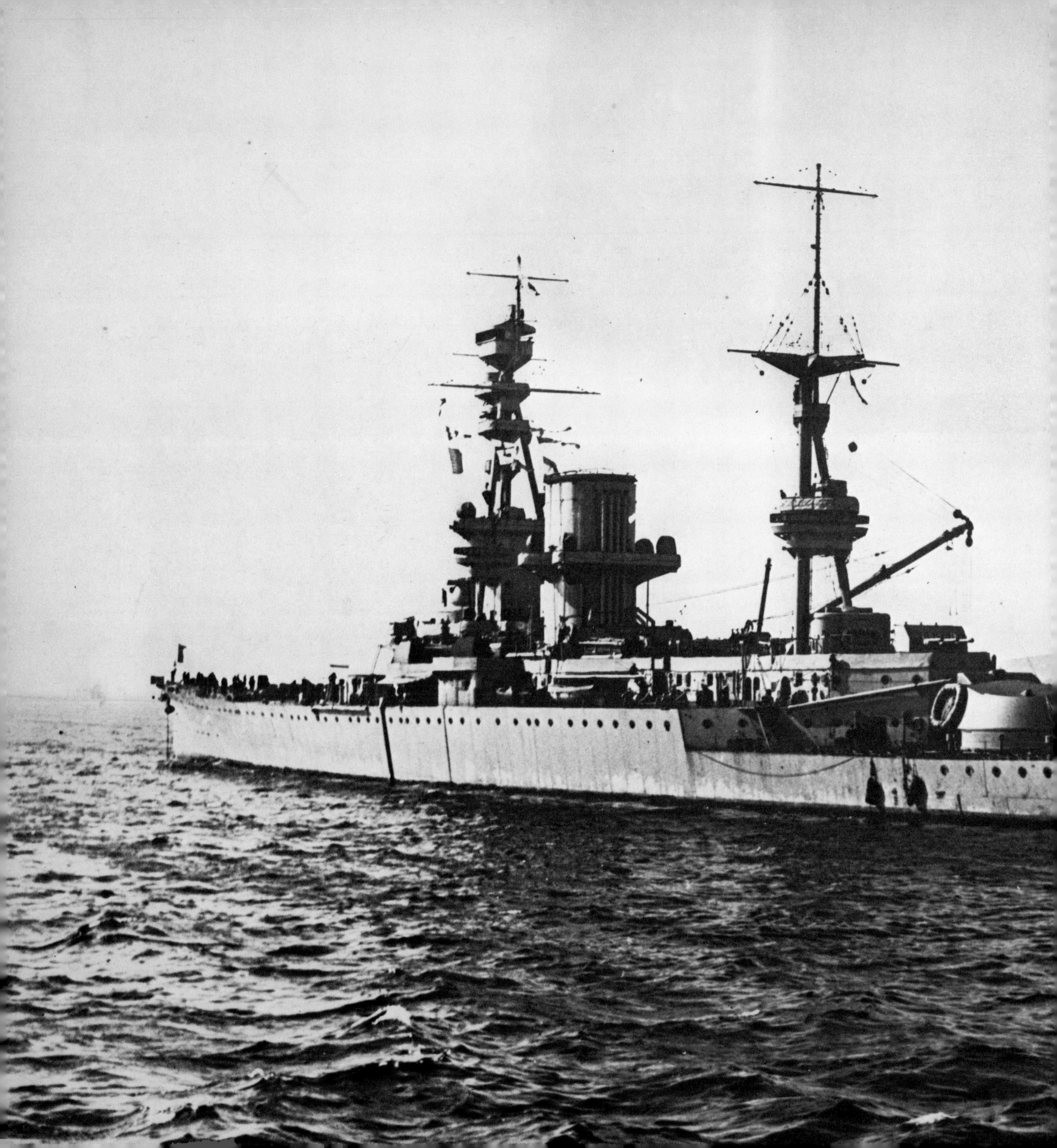

Above: *Glorious* in Scapa Flow, c.1917/18. She and her sister were strange-looking vessels, with their large, single funnel, extremely long, flared hull and 15in turrets fore and aft.
Left: *Courageous* at Scapa Flow in December 1916. The vessels of the class were almost identical, but the searchlight platform around the funnel was staggered in *Glorious* and on one level in *Courageous*.

COURAGEOUS CLASS

Name of ship:	*Courageous*	*Glorious*
Builder(s):	Armstrongs, Elswick	Harland and Wolff
Laid down:	28 March 1915	1 May 1915
Launched:	5 February 1916	20 April 1916
Completed:	January 1917	January 1917

Displacement
Normal condition: 18,580 tons
Deep load: 22,560 tons

Dimensions
Length: 735ft (between perpendiculars); 786ft (overall)
Beam: 81ft
Draught: 22ft 1¼in (normal); 25ft 10in (deep)

Armament (as completed)
4-15in 42-calibre
18-4in
2-3in high angle AA
7 machine-guns
6-21in torpedo tubes

Armour protection
Main belt: 3in-2in
Bulkheads: 3in-2in
Barbettes: 7in-3in
Turrets: 13in-11in
Conning tower: 10in
Forecastle: 1in
Upper deck: 1in
Main deck: ¾in-1¾in (between barbettes)
Lower deck: 1½in-3in (over steering gear)

Machinery
Parsons geared turbines driving four screws
18 Yarrow small-tubed boilers
90,000shp for speed of 31-32 knots

Fuel and endurance
750 tons of oil (minimum); 3,160 tons (maximum)
Endurance: 3,200 miles at 19 knots

Complement
829-842

Fate(s)
Both ships were lost in action in the early years of the Second World War. *Courageous* fell victim to a U-boat attack on 17 September 1939 and was sunk after being hit by at least two torpedoes. *Glorious* was attacked and sunk by gunfire from *Scharnhorst* and *Gneisenau* on 8 June 1940.

Note
Courageous and *Glorious* were an odd pair; completed as battlecruisers these vessels were really only light cruisers with battleship armament which, when fired, shook the hull badly. It was decided that neither had a place in the Grand Fleet and, after the end of the First World War, they were converted as aircraft carriers, a role in which they proved extremely successful.

Top: *Glorious* with units of the Grand Fleet in Scapa Flow, 1917. On 17 November 1917, *Glorious*, in company with *Repulse* and *Courageous* and screened by a force of light cruisers and destroyers, was in action with units of the German High Seas Fleet who were at the time protecting their own minesweepers off Kattegat. Nothing came of the action, with the German force quickly escaping without serious damage. The worst damage sustained in the action was caused by the blast from the 15in guns of *Courageous* and *Glorious*, which scarred their own decks!
Right: The battlecruiser *Glorious* undergoing steam trials upon completion in 1916. On discovery of hull strain revealed during their early trials, the *Courageous* class were returned to the dockyards to have extra strengthening pillars and 'Z-bar' supports fitted. *Glorious* and her sister *Courageous* were two of the oddest ships built during the dreadnought period. Although officially rated as large, light cruisers, they did not fit naturally into any role as they were too lightly armoured for work in the battle-line yet too large to be effective in the cruiser role.
Far right: *Glorious* in 1918, fitted with new searchlight towers around the funnel and on the mainmast. Note the aircraft on 'B' turret.

91

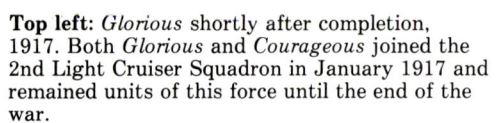

Top left: *Glorious* shortly after completion, 1917. Both *Glorious* and *Courageous* joined the 2nd Light Cruiser Squadron in January 1917 and remained units of this force until the end of the war.
Top right: *Furious* in 1917. A strange vessel, she was originally designed as a large, light cruiser and then altered while under construction to carry one single 18in gun aft with the forecastle completely dedicated to aircraft. She was used as a minelayer for a short period after completion.
Below: A starboard broadside shot of *Furious* in 1917. Her main role in this guise was confined to experiments with aircraft take-offs and landings, both of which proved hazardous because of the relatively short runway forward.

FURIOUS

Builder(s): Armstrongs, Elswick
Laid down: June 1915
Launched: 15 August 1916
Completed: July 1917

Displacement
Normal condition: 19,513 tons
Deep load: 22,890 tons

Dimensions
Length: 750ft (waterline); 786ft 6in (overall)
Beam: 88ft
Draught: 24ft (normal); 26ft 6in (deep)

Armament (as completed)
2-18in 40-calibre (as designed, but only fitted with aft gun)
11-5.5in
2-3in high angle AA
4-3pdr
4-21in torpedo tubes above water
2-21in torpedo tubes submerged

Armour protection
Main belt: 3in-2in over 1in plating
Bulkheads: 2in-3in
Barbettes: 7in-4in
Turrets: 13in faces, 11in rears
Conning tower: 10in
Forecastle: 1in
Upper deck: 1in
Main deck: ¾in-1¾in
Lower: 1½in-3in

Machinery
Brown and Curtis geared turbines, driving four screws
18 Yarrow small-tubed boilers, providing 94,000shp

Fuel and endurance
750 tons of oil (minimum); 3,160 tons (maximum)
Endurance: 11,000 miles at economical speed, 12 knots

Complement
880, as part carrier

Fate(s)
After a long, active career, *Furious* was scrapped from 1948.

Note
Furious was designed as the ultimate in big-gun vessels, although she was mounted on a ridiculously light cruiser frame. Only the aft single 18in gun was mounted, but when fired it threatened to split the ship apart — an experience that was described as very unpleasant. The forward part of the ship was converted into a flight deck and was partially successful. After the war she was fully converted as a carrier and was successful in that role, emulating the *Courageous* class, which were the world's first true aircraft carriers.

94

The following views are of the once mighty battlefleet under the scrapper's torch.

Left: *Resolution* at Devonport on 23 August 1947, shortly before cutting commenced. Alongside *Resolution* are the Battle class destroyer *Dunkirk* and Bangor class minesweeper *Bridport*.

Far left and below left: *Revenge* at Inverkeithing, Scotland in the hands of Thomas Ward & Co., Shipbreakers, 1949. She is seen having her foretop dismantled.

Top: *Revenge*, with her 15in guns severed, crashing to the deck. Note how the guns are cut into small sections to facilitate removal.

Middle: *Warspite* aground on the rocks at Prussia Cove, Cornwall, having cheated the breakers yard after parting her tow rope en route in rough weather. When it became known publicly that *Warspite* was for the scrapyard, there was a call for the vessel to be saved and preserved as a museum ship, because she was perhaps the most famous of British battleships. Alas, despite strong protests, she was condemned to the same fate as her sister-ships.

Below: *Warspite* reduced to scrap as she lies on the rocks, June 1950. Her remnants could be seen as late as 1956.

Top left: The bow of *Valiant*, May 1950. *Valiant* was scrapped at Cairnryan in Scotland by Arnott Young, although her hulk was transferred to Troon for final demolition in March 1950.
Top right: *Valiant's* stern, 1950.
Centre right: *Ramillies*, her bows quickly vanishing, November 1949. She was scrapped by Arnott Young Ltd. at Cairnryan from 20 February 1948.
Below right: *Resolution's* hulk, 6 July 1949.